LONDON

The

GREENWICH
MARKET

Cookbook

EST. 1737

by the traders of Greenwich Market

Introduction by Rebecca Seal
Photography by Colin Hampden-White
Illustrations by Kath van Uytrecht

KITCHEN PRESS

First published in the UK in 2016 by
Kitchen Press Ltd
1 Windsor Place
Dundee
DD2 1BG

ISBN 9780957037380
A catalogue record for this book is available from the British Library

Printed in the UK by Bell & Bain Ltd

ACKNOWLEDGEMENTS

The publisher would like to thank all the Greenwich Market traders for sharing both their recipes and their positivity. Special thanks also to Gillie Bexson and Anna Rakitina at Greenwich Hospital, Jennifer Hall-Thompson at Proactive PR; market managers Ben Niblett and Alex Gillespie; Jessie Levene for both her Mandarin and her culinary prowess; Guiseppe Lambertino for helping out with the Italian, Jenny Wheatley for getting an unruly manuscript into shape, Laura Curry and Jane Adams for their thorough recipe testing and Andrew Forteath for his great design work.

Greenwich Hospital
Supporting the Royal Navy since 1694

Greenwich Hospital is Britain's oldest Royal Naval charity. It provides charitable support to serving and retired personnel of the Royal Navy and Royal Marines and their dependents including annuities, sheltered housing and educational bursaries and grants. The funds are raised from the Charity's investment portfolio. In 2015 Greenwich Hospital gave £7.4m in grants, charitable payments and educational support to over 25,000 beneficiaries through more than thirty Royal Navy and Tri-Service charities.

Greenwich Estate is the land originally transferred to the first Greenwich Hospital Commissioners pursuant to the Royal Charter of 1694 by which Greenwich Hospital was founded. This, with other land acquired subsequently, forms the site of the historic Greenwich Hospital buildings and the nucleus of the Maritime Greenwich World Heritage Site. The Estate subsequently acquired the site of much of what is now the commercial centre of Greenwich surrounding the Market area.

www.grenhosp.org.uk
www.greenwichmarketlondon.com

CONTENTS

INTRODUCTION

Stand on the cobbled floor of Greenwich Market and close your eyes. Listen to the hubbub and chatter. Listen to awnings flapping against poles, traders laughing, boxes of vegetables being trundled in from the street outside, to the meat sizzling on grills and a hundred conversations in a dozen different languages. Many of the sounds you will hear today are no different to those you would have heard 300 years ago, when the market was first granted a Royal Charter. The stall-holders may now be selling hand-pulled noodles, pancakes or chai, but they still call out from stall to stall, teasing each other about how much they've sold and sharing their food at the end of the day. They may be making dim sum, pad Thai or doughnuts, but the scent of the market hasn't changed much either. The hot, sweet, smoky, sharp tangs of the food market mingle together to create something which is at once unique to this place, on this day, while also being common to all food markets, throughout time.

The name Greenwich comes from the Old English for green harbour and so, since its very earliest days, Greenwich has been somewhere for newcomers to disembark, and for new ingredients to be traded. For centuries, the market and the narrow lanes and streets which surround it have been a hub for traders offering spices, meat, fish, sugar, fruit and vegetables. Then, just as today, the fringes of the market were occupied by hostelries and small shops selling woodwork, glass and china; then, like now, the distinctive intonations of born-and-bred south Londoners would merge with accents from all over the known world.

Greenwich is both part of London, and a town in its own right, with its own particular character. The area has been settled since the Bronze Age, with evidence of Saxon and Roman life here too. With a deep-water river harbour on a curve of the Thames and a gently sloping hill leading away from the water, it has provided a safe and productive haven for communities for millennia – although it has also seen its fair share of strife: Viking raiders liked its seclusion and moored their boats at Greenwich while conducting raids on Canterbury and London.

By the 15th century, Greenwich was home to the Tudors, England's royal family at the time, who built a palace on the banks of the river; Henry VIII was born here, held one of his many marriages in the palace, and his daughters, Mary, Queen of Scots and Elizabeth I, were born here too. A tree in Greenwich Park is known as Queen Elizabeth's Oak because she used to play in its branches as a child. During the 16th and 17th centuries, the Stuarts, England's next royal family, began work on a new residence, demolishing parts of the old palace, but work had barely started when they decided to move upstream, to be closer to central London. The site was rarely used until 1694, when Queen Mary II decided to create a Royal Hospital for Seamen. Within three months of its formal establishment, the queen sadly died aged just 32. Her husband, King William III, decided to continue with the project in memory of his wife.

The beautiful buildings now standing just metres from the market were mostly designed by Sir Christopher Wren and his assistant Nicholas Hawksmoor, and are often referred to as the Old Royal Naval College or simply as the Maritime Buildings. Originally, though, they were built to house more than 2,500 seamen who were too old, injured or ill to work for the Navy any longer. Today, Greenwich Hospital is the largest naval charity and still owns all these grand, pale stone buildings – now used by the National Maritime Museum, Greenwich University and Trinity Laban College of Music; the old brewery and bakery which fed and watered the pensioners has been re-opened as a bar and restaurant. The rent received from the modern market, the shops and houses around it and the Old Royal Navel College buildings provide Greenwich Hospital with an income for its charitable works.

In the 1830s Greenwich Hospital decided to move the market a few metres west, to its current location, now known as the island. It constructed a purpose-built market place surrounded by wide streets, with a public house on two of its four corners, and a music hall and theatre above the arched entrance. This was expensive so, in 1849, Parliament gave the Hospital new powers to charge stall-holders rent and tolls, and allowed the market to take place twice a week. By 1905 the market was busily running six days a week, but just a few years later the slaughterhouses and stables, which had dealt with livestock as well as horses for transport, saw a sharp decline in trade. For the next seven decades, the market concentrated on fruit and vegetables – you can still see some of the shutter-fronted storage units the traders used on the edge of the market. (One of the pubs, the Coach and Horses, had a 24-hour licence when the fruit and veg market was at its busiest – much of the trading was done in the early hours of the morning and some traders lived a mostly nocturnal existence.) Gradually, Greenwich was eclipsed by other, bigger produce markets and Greenwich Hospital took the difficult decision to close it and convert the storage units into little shops. In 1985 the market re-opened as an arts and crafts market, first just at weekends and, as its reputation grew, by the year 2000 demand was high enough to once again open during the week too.

About a decade ago Greenwich Hospital realised that the thousands who flocked to the island to buy antiques, art, pottery and woodwork, would probably welcome the chance to buy edible treats as well. (Coincidentally, this was when I first moved nearby – a visit to the market followed by a pint in one of the market's atmospheric pubs became a weekend ritual.) Cheese, olives, bread and cake stalls arrived first. Three years later, the first hot food traders arrived, including Jay Hong, who still runs one of the market's most beloved stalls, Teriyaki-ya. 'We are one of the oldest traders in the market,' he says. 'We were one of just a few stalls at the very beginning, then other traders began to join us: Chinese, Brazilian, Thai, Ethiopian and Turkish. Every week a few more would be invited in and everything you see now grew from there.'

Many of those early traders still trade at the market, like the Louisiana Hot Dog stall and Hot Flavours Caribbean food. A crêpe stall was quickly followed by one selling churros, and the Red Cow Carvery arrived soon after, with their famous roast beef sandwiches and Yorkshire puddings. The market's management team – which has the enviable task of overseeing which stalls appear at the market – is always looking for traders who can bring something scrumptious as well as different to the table, whether beautiful, juicy sausages, perfect Spanish tapas, or squidgy brownies still warm from the oven. About a quarter of the market, once focused on entirely craft and art, is now dedicated to food.

Like other London markets in places like Brixton or Hackney, Greenwich is part of the huge street-food trend which has travelled across the Atlantic from Los Angeles, San Francisco and New York. Five or six years ago, street food was barely acknowledged in the UK, but now we are all – happily – much more familiar with the idea of eating food from around the world, tasting dishes that are served from carts, vans and road-side kitchens everywhere from the Americas to Asia. It's no surprise then, that the food served in Greenwich is full of international flavour. If you ask the traders where their dishes come from, the list of influences is dizzying: 'My ramen burgers were inspired by some I tasted in New York,' says Harry Delos Santos from Pimp My Ramen, who is from the Philippines. 'But I serve up my very own recipe with lots of Filipino flavours as well as a touch of Japanese and a dollop of American.' Elika Ashoori, who runs Lilika's Treats, says, 'Many of the flavours for my macarons and cakes draw on my Iranian heritage, such as rose, pistachio and pomegranate, and I use honey to sweeten instead of sugar.' And Emmanuel La Gona – who is from Venezuela – and Joanez Brusco – who is from Brazil, say the inspiration for their stall, Munchies, has a South American twist. 'Our speciality is a Cuban sandwich but we marinade our pulled pork in habanero chillies (hot!), herbs, pickles and mustard and then layer in bread with smoked ham and Monterey Jack cheese.'

In a busy week, the whole market can see up to 150 stall-holders in action. There are the antiques and collectables on some days and the designer-makers on others; each day features a different mix of traders and that's what makes it so vibrant. Although many are local to Greenwich, some come from Kent or even as far as Wiltshire, drawn in by the distinctive community spirit which permeates the market, and – as many traders often comment – the wonderful array of food available to eat during their working days, whether they choose curry from India or Ethiopia, Scotch eggs or a plateful of moreish empanadas.

Unsurprisingly, there is fierce competition for a spot in the food market, and requests to join arrive all the time. In fact, it's even more attractive to traders now, as the recent enhancement works to the market mean it has a new roof, re-laid cobbles and a stand-alone food court area to one side in Fry's Court for very busy days. This luxurious position means that the market can also host night-time events, and assures its future as a foodie destination.

Greenwich is packed with amazing museums which attract millions of tourists every year, like the restored Cutty Sark, once the fastest tea clipper in the world, displayed in a dry dock on the waterside; the Observatory and Meridian Line and the National Maritime Museum amongst others. But the market is as much for locals as it is for passing visitors – in fact, most of the buildings on the island house residents in the floors above the market itself. It is there to serve everyone, whether they are foodie pilgrims, crossing London – or the country – to try a new dish (I'm looking at you and your legion of followers, Pimp My Ramen!), the people living nearby who come with their kids on a Sunday, or those who work around Greenwich in the week.

This sense of community is shared by the food traders too. 'Working here is like being in someone's home, it's not simply a market,' says David Barnini, of Italian stall Imbert Street Food. Jamie from Turnips, a shop and stall selling fresh juices and grilled cheese sandwiches agrees. 'It's like a family here. The market is a community – some other markets aren't as community-spirited.' Michaela Pontiki from Arapina, a Greek-influenced pâtisserie stall, feels the same. 'The best things about working here are the atmosphere and the relationship we have with our fellow traders.' For Enzo Moschetta, from Saint Sugar of London, the diversity of the market and its visitors is part of the reason he loves coming to work. 'I like the contact with different traders and customers from all over the world.'

And it's not just a close community – it's a creative community too, embracing businesses beyond the food world. Many of the designer-maker shops that surround the market started life as arts and craft stalls on the market itself. Julia Johnson has been part of the market for forty years, ever since her parents established Pickwick Papers and Fabrics, their shop on the southern edge of the island, which she now runs. 'We are all creative here,' she says. 'Apart from fabrics and colour, my other passion is food – I love being able to pop out and get freshly made sushi, or a beautiful box of halloumi and salad. I use the food market far, far too much!'

For Fay Aykiran from Victus & Bibo (whose Turkish lamb and halloumi wraps have a cult following), the combination of art and food was part of the reason she and her partner, Eddie, chose to join the market in 2005. 'Such talented individuals, so many brilliant artists, all in one area, can only give off an explosion of energy,' she says. 'The ambience of the market has always been so awesome, with the buzz of people coming in and out of the space and traders from different cultures and backgrounds.' The area itself also drew them in. 'We are both from south-east London, and Greenwich has always been close to our hearts. As children we both experienced river walks during school holidays, the Cutty Sark, the park on snowy and sunny days. The history behind the Naval College was always embedded in our minds – so what better place to start your business than in an area you have such fond memories of?'

X

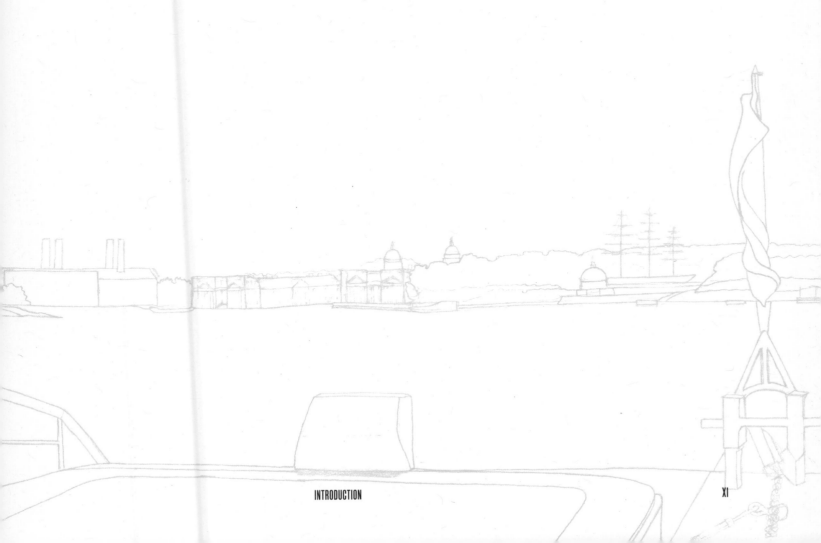

And what better place to create a cookbook? As a way of celebrating the history of this ancient market as well as the dynamic and delicious place it has become, a collection of recipes is hard to beat. Recipes look like simple things, but in every blend of ingredients there is a hidden story – the story of how a trader came to be making this dish, in this market; or the story of a nationality and the pride its people take in sharing the food they eat. This compilation of recipes is as individual as the place that brought them together – where else would you find Ethiopian lentils, Jamaican curry goat, yoghurt gelato, star anise and cayenne truffles, Argentinian chimichurri, chicken kofte meatballs and saffron rice pudding all bubbling happily along together? I, for one, can't wait to tuck in.

Rebecca Seal
London, September 2015

NOTES ON TEMPERATURES, WEIGHTS AND MEASURES

OVEN TEMPERATURES

All temperatures in the recipes are for a standard electric oven. If you're cooking in a fan oven, you should lower the temperature by about 20ºC. If you've got a gas oven, check the chart below for conversions.

ºC	Gas Mark
140	1
150	2
170	3
180	4
190	5
200	6
220	7
230	8
240	9

WEIGHTS AND MEASURES

All the weights and measures in the book are in metric. All eggs are large unless stated otherwise, and should preferably be free-range and organic. Butter is salted unless stated otherwise.

Most of the measurements are precise and straightforward, but produce comes in different shapes and sizes so often recipes will refer to 'a medium potato' or 'a handful of flat-leaf parsley'. Your hands may be bigger than the traders', so don't worry too much and put in what you feel is going to work: you'll end up making it according to your own taste and that is really what it's all about.

NOTES ON CONTRIBUTORS

A market, by definition, is a fluid thing – a group of traders that, in Greenwich, changes its make-up by the day. Over the eighteen-month period that it took to research and collate this book, new traders have pitched up and some old ones have moved on or taken a break from market life. This is a snapshot of the food market as it was in 2014–2015.

ARAPINA

The idea for Michaela Pontiki's business came from a family recipe for chocolate cake dating back to 1937. As a twenty-five-year-old who had recently become vegetarian, she was looking for a way to make dairy-free cakes with all natural, unprocessed ingredients. She is Greek, with a family heritage that stretches back to the Greek communities in Asia Minor, and she brings that Mediterranean inspiration to her cooking – the first Arapina cake is based on an old Cretan recipe that uses olive oil. Michaela says, 'My mum had a big influence on me as I was growing up. For me, baking brings back the smells of orange and cinnamon in our kitchen all those years ago, and I always try to bring that loving feeling to my baking.' Increasingly, she is experimenting with raw cakes and with creating dairy-free, sugar-free, gluten-free treats – healthier, lighter, but sacrificing nothing in terms of flavour.

ARAWAK GRILL

Robert Robinson has worked in kitchens all his adult life, from being a Terence Conran apprentice to moving to the oil town of Aberdeen and giving a bit of Caribbean fire to the Scots – with a stint as a tour DJ in the middle. But his true inspiration is the diverse cultures and flavours of Jamaica – not for nothing is the island's motto 'Out of Many, One'. He calls his own family 'the united colours of Benetton' because they have roots in so many places – China, Africa, Asia and Europe – and it's that cultural twist that he brings to his cooking. The sound of 'stamp and go' frying up behind his stall and the deep spicy smell of his curry goat is tantalising. He and his brother Stephen bring the tastes of Jamaica bang up to date and it's hard to resist as you walk past.

L'ARTISAN

Now sadly closed, L'Artisan was a deli on Greenwich's Trafalgar Road and a sometime stall on the market, selling wonderful pies, cakes, stews and whatever else owner Dustin Louw felt like cooking up. His passion is for French food and for showing people how to cook. As a boy in South Africa, he says, all food was made at home from family recipes – a social experience, full of love. That's what makes it taste good, right? It's that love, that passion, that he carried into his dishes – famously pressing the recipe for boeuf Bourguignon on customers who said how much they loved his, or encouraging them to make their own pastry from scratch.

BÁNH MÌ NÊN

Ngoc Thanh Tran is from the city of Ho Chi Minh and made his way to London via Sydney. He was only intending to stay for a year while he studied tourism, but a day trip to Greenwich changed everything: 'I was so excited to see the street food market in Greenwich and there was not any Vietnamese food stall yet, so I came up with the idea to run a business in London, introducing Vietnamese foods to many tourists and local people in the famous tourist destination.' He's been here ever since, serving bánh mì – the addictive Vietnamese take on a chicken baguette – and fresh summer rolls to a dedicated clientele.

BLACK VANILLA

A café on College Approach, Black Vanilla is a more sophisticated gelateria than most. Downstairs are the gelato cabinets, where the flavours change seasonally and can range from black forest gâteau gelato to Pimm's and lemonade sorbetto via panettone gelato, depending on the time of year. You can take your cone out, or ask to have it upstairs in the small Georgian rooms that have been converted into an elegant sitting area; somewhere for a bit of respite from the bustle of the market and to drink one of their excellent coffees, or a signature gelato cocktail. Susan Stretch started off her career as a barrister, but when she had children was inspired to set up her own business and fit it around her family life – perhaps not predicting quite how successful her ice cream parlour would become. Now Black Vanilla has two branches (in Greenwich and Blackheath), sells through Ocado and cinemas and theatres throughout the UK and makes bespoke ice cream for a whole host of partners.

BLOWING DANDELION

The Blowing Dandelion stall is a real beauty to behold. Michaela's iridescent chocolates are moulded like cut jewels or perfect gleaming spheres and are dusted with shimmering metallic colours. They look both futuristic and Art Deco at once, and have been described as 'tiny edible galaxies'. The truffles inside, however, taste anything but futuristic: they are smooth and luxurious with over thirty pure, deep flavours like Aztec truffle, cherry moon, sloe gin or lime and chilli. Michaela is Slovakian, but these chocolates have no cultural background other than her imagination.

BONBON CAFÉ

Grace Crump has been making jams since she was a child, first using hedgerow blackberries. When she was bringing up her children, she would make jam with whatever fruit she could get her hands on – whether foraged, grown in her own garden or begged from neighbours – and give jars away to friends and family. They were so popular, that an idea for a business started to take hold… Originally from the Caribbean island of Antigua, there are sometimes hints of the tropical flavours in her jams, but Grace's true passion is using seasonal local produce to create small batches of her jewel-like preserves. Jellies, jams, marmalades and chutneys – all made in her own kitchen with no preservatives or added colour. A piece of toast, laden with melted butter and her blackberry jelly is truly worth giving a bit of time and attention to.

BUENOS AIRES CAFÉ

The team behind Buenos Aires Café is a pretty diverse one: head chef Reinaldo Vargas was a dancer and paparazzo, wife Kate worked in retail and brother-in-law Martin Dunford was one of the founders of *Rough Guides*. Between the three of them, they've created two perfect pockets of Argentina in Greenwich and Blackheath. The Greenwich café lies on Nelson Road just behind the market and serves up a myriad of cuts of Argentine beef, empanadas, at least four different kinds of their own homemade chorizo and the classic chimichurri sauce. There is a huge European influence in Argie culture – around fifty-five per cent of the population is Italian in origin, and this influence carries through to the cuisine, too – so pasta, gnocchi and pizza are everyday foods. BA Café do a mean pizza and silky homemade pastas: tortelli come filled with butternut squash and sage or wild mushrooms, or you can have ravioli with smoked salmon or spinach and ricotta. They also have list of Argentine wines you'd be hard pushed to better in Buenos Aires itself. It's an easy place to sit and while away an hour or so, watching the people go by and dreaming you're in warmer climes.

CHAMPAGNE + FROMAGE

Standing at the Church Street entrance to the market, Champagne + Fromage offers pretty much the perfect bistro experience. The vast list of limited-production, fine-quality Champagne is all sourced from small, family-owned vineyards, each with their own personality and heritage, and all served by the glass which gives a wonderful opportunity to explore, compare and contrast. The menu serves up the very best in French bistro classics but the thing to focus on is the cheese. The tartines are wonderful – slices of chewy, toasted country bread topped with, say, melted Langres cheese and sautéed pear, or figs on top of a bubbling slice of *Fourme d'Ambert*. You can also choose your own selection for a cheese board – they stock over fifty varieties of cheese from all over France – and then get the expert staff to tell you which Champagnes to drink with it. All in all a very civilised, and civilising, experience.

COOPIE-COCO

Alshon Higgins has an eccentric stall at Greenwich. Most of the table is taken up by bowlfuls of his wonderfully big, craggy, hand-formed chocolate truffles, dusty with cocoa and full of deep dark flavours. They are pretty hard to look past, but ignore his other goods at your peril, for here you'll find some true Jamaican specialities like coconut drops, gizzadas and extremely delicious and savoury

Jamaican patties. Alshon learnt to cook from his Grandma when he went to live with her in the Jamaican parish of Saint Mary as a child. She'd cook for everyone, and anyone passing through the village could drop in and expect a little treat from her kitchen. Her legacy is alive in Alshon's food, whether in the tropical spicing of his chocolates or his faithful renditions of her dishes.

ETHIOPIAN VEGETARIAN FOOD

Ethiopian food is little known in London outside very particular enclaves of the city, and Helen Partridge is doing a great job of changing that. Her stall is crazily colourful, packed with different pans simmering away, and pays homage to the strong vegetarian tradition in Ethiopian cooking: chickpeas in tomato sauce; lentils, beans, samosas and soups; often served in the spongy flatbread *injera*. In an Ethiopian market it would all be cooked over an open fire, absorbing smoky flavours as it simmered away, while here in her adopted homeland market managers aren't as relaxed so she makes do with a gas ring – but that's about the only difference.

FORNO VIAGGIANTE PIZZERIA

Giancarlo's beautiful old Citroën van produces the most wonderful aromas when it's parked up at Greenwich. Complete with wood-fired stone oven, the van serves some of the best and most authentic pizzas you will ever have tasted, with a kaleidoscopic and ever-changing array of toppings. Giancarlo has been making pizza ever since he arrived in the UK from his native town of Napoli. He was initially depressed when he saw what was served up as pizza here, but he learnt the methods of the pizza maestros back home and set up his own business bringing real Neapolitan pizza to the people of London. He uses 100 per cent Italian wheat flour and a slow rise to make crusts that are blistered and charred in the heat of the oven. Toppings can range from the classic margherita to his own more elaborate inventions like the marvellous 'mosaico' with mozzarella, kale and anchovies.

GOOD FORTUNE CHINESE FOOD

Originally from Liaoning Province in north-east China, Jinggang Wang abandoned a career in IT to run his Greenwich-based business. His biggest influence, he says, is his mother's cooking from his childhood and you can taste that home-style attention to detail in his dishes – which perhaps explains the queue of Chinese students waiting for his food, looking for the authentic taste of home. His dishes range from brilliantly executed classics – a sticky, tangy sweet and sour pork, for example – to the lesser known spicy specialities of Hunan. It's definitely worth ordering outside your comfort zone.

GREENWICH COOKIE TIME

Thomas Stevens, aka Greenwich Cookie Time, is a mysterious entity. All we know about him is that he makes the tenderest crumbed cookies – from choc chip to snickerdoodle – which are the perfect end to a lunch on the hoof around the market. Search him out – he's quite self-effacing but his biscuits are most certainly not.

HOLA PAELLA

Hola Paella used to occupy a shop facing the market which was a treasure trove of deliciousness. Famous for the vast pans of paella they cooked outside the shopfront, inside they stocked an extraordinary display of Spanish produce which chef Carrie Mueller showcased in salads and cold tapas on the deli counter. All is not lost though – while the shop is temporarily closed, Hola Paella still have a stall at the market selling paella and tapas. Carrie describes her dishes as 'simple but big tasting', inspired by Iberian flavours, her mum and by her travels around the globe – and she makes one of the best gazpachos you can eat outside Spain.

IMBERT STREET FOOD

Serving up hand-crafted, traditional Italian pastas in simple but gutsy sauces – that's what Imbert Street Food is all about. Marco Toran and David Barnini come from Puglia and Tuscany respectively, and they believe that 'to do something good, we have to come back to the origin'. Everything is prepared just as their grandmothers would cook it and a box of their food can set any chilly day to rights – always piled high and piping hot and covered with really good Parmesan cheese. Ravioli with tomato sauce and beef meatballs, gnocchi with gorgonzola and cream, and ricotta and spinach ravioli with pesto are regulars, but if you're lucky you'll also find arancini – those deep-fried, pointed rice balls stuffed with mozzarella and spinach or Bolognese, or whatever is good that day.

LA-MIAN & DIM SUM

The La-Mian & Dim Sum stall is a quiet legend in London street food circles. Husband and wife Liu Zhongyi and Shi Haixian (aka Kelly) met in London but are both originally from north-east China – a land of freezing winters tempered by a hearty, wheat-based cuisine. La-Mian & Dim Sum proffers a tempting photo menu that combines these traditional northern Chinese foods (including the stall's signature la-mian – hand-pulled wheat noodles in a rich meat broth) with the southern, more well known tradition of dim sum – delicate steamed dumplings, often with a seafood filling. One of only a few places in London serving authentic la-mian, Zhongyi learnt to make the dish from his father and uncle. As they would in China, Zhongyi makes the noodles within eyesight of his customers. Through a theatrical process of twisting, folding, pulling and loud slapping of the dough onto the worktop, Zhongyi creates perfect noodles from raw dough in mere minutes. He also makes it look ridiculously easy, which it certainly is not. The noodles are then served in a delicious broth made from chicken, beef and pork bones, cooked for three hours with a variety of Chinese spices, and finished with your choice of topping – Zhongyi's favourite is the beef, while Kelly prefers the sour spicy version.

LE LEMURIEN

Lilia is from Madagascar, and is proud to be one of the only people making Madagascan food in London. Back home, her grandmother would cook for over thirty people every weekend, and now Lilia carries that tradition forwards: 'There are only 2,000 Madagascan people in the UK, and I'm the only one doing Madagascan street food. I make things like ginger or coconut chicken; lasary, which is cabbage and carrot spiced with dried lemon, chilli, ginger, onion and turmeric; tangy French beans cooked with vinegar, lemon and salt; Indian-style lentils served over rice... Madagascan food has been influenced by Europe, India, China and Africa, so there's a huge mix of flavours.' Her dahl is milky and smooth, the perfect foil for her soured cabbage and bean dishes. Her coconut chicken takes pieces of chicken thigh, and chars them on a flat grill, so they are tender and crispy and sweet all at once – treat yourself.

LILIKA'S TREATS

Elika Ashkoori has been selling macarons, cheesecakes, brownies and more at Greenwich Market for just over a year, but in that short time she's made herself a vital cog in the machine. It's not just that her stall is pretty as a picture, with rows of macarons in every flavour and colour imaginable (think kiwi, peanut butter, lemon, blackberry) and slabs of cheesecake from strawberry to crème brûlée. It's not just that she has a very light hand with baking and all her goods taste outrageously delicious. It's that she also brings a bit of communal sunshine with her whenever she trades – an indefatigable Tweeter and Facebooker, she is a committed promoter of the market and keeps up a steady stream of photographs of all the personalities and stalls that appear there. She's well worth a follow for updates from the very heart of the market.

MOGUL

Mogul sits at the Greenwich Church Street entrance to the market, and is rooted in the food culture of the Punjab in north India. A Greenwich institution for the last twenty years, it is spread over three floors of a seventeenth century townhouse and comprises an upstairs private dining room, a ground floor bar and restaurant and an intimate cellar restaurant. The ground floor is a particularly civilised place to sit for a couple of hours, with its cool, elegant décor and picture windows through which you can watch the world go by. Head chef, Mr PD Khan, is from Delhi and trained in two of the finest hotels there, the Oberoi and the Sheraton. Everything here is made from scratch, and he insists on using freshly ground herbs and spices so the flavours in his dishes sing with authenticity.

MUNCHIES

The Munchies burrito stall is the one you are happiest to find when you are really truly very hungry. Owners Rebecca George, Emmanuel La Gona and Joanez Brusco are from Wales, Venezuela and Brazil respectively, and together they share a passion for the food and culture of Latin America. Their food is richly flavoured, spicy and colourful – burritos on offer might include anything from shredded chicken and pomegranate to roasted vegetables to Venezuelan beef pabellón, and are packed with extras like rice, beans, cabbage, cheese and avocado. And hot sauce – don't forget the hot sauce! They have an unbelievable collection of chilli sauces from all over the Americas and say they love it so much that they have been known to cook food to complement their favourite sauces instead of choosing sauce to complement the food.

NO. 57A

No. 57A serves artisan wraps and is the brainchild of Italian couple Matteo and Marzia. Matteo is from the northern region of Fruili Venezia Giulia, Marzia hails from Sicily, and while their food has a strong Italian influence they have also taken inspiration from the melting pot that is London. Their wonderfully fluffy, chewy flatbreads are made with Indian chapati flour and are cooked fresh on their griddle while you wait. Some of the fillings are classically Italian – meatballs in tomato sauce, mortadella – but their best seller is a tender, juicy barbecue pulled pork straight from the USA. They've put a lot of love and soul into everything about their stall – from the hand-painted logo to the old marble slab they roll out the bread dough on – and you can taste it in every wrap.

PIG DOGS AND BRISKET

Kelvin Sturman has form in the food world – twenty years' experience as a chef, partner and MD of a restaurant and hotel group – but he's packed in the formal arena of fine dining for a more freewheeling existence selling slow-smoked Southern street food. His beautiful 1965 Citroën HY van has been converted to house an American barbecue smoker, which he fires up to smoke brisket and pork belly over hickory chips. His inspiration was a 15,000-mile gastronomic road trip across the US, where he discovered the delights of the barbecue pits in Texas, Tennessee, Kansas and the Carolinas. Those flavours stayed with him when he came back to the UK, and he started to experiment with a few Asian twists. He serves up his perfectly smoked meat with home-pickled watermelon or Asian salad in soft, fresh brioche rolls to make a really unmissable sandwich.

PIMP MY RAMEN

Possibly one of the more unlikely success stories of the market, Harry Delos Santos reckons he is the only person in the UK selling ramen burgers and he has got a cult following for doing it. What is a ramen burger? The classic is a beef patty, topped with cheese and a fried egg, and sandwiched between two fried ramen 'buns' – crispy on the outside, soft and slippery on the inside, and incredibly tasty and messy to eat. Other equally delicious options are chicken teriyaki and an amazing Filipino pulled pork – and he also does a vitamin-packed vegetarian burger made from sweet potato, white rice, chickpeas and spinach. As a meal it's hard to categorise – sort of Asian, sort of Filipino, sort of American – but it's definitely 100 per cent pimped.

PLANET PANCAKE

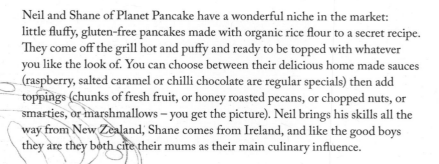

Neil and Shane of Planet Pancake have a wonderful niche in the market: little fluffy, gluten-free pancakes made with organic rice flour to a secret recipe. They come off the grill hot and puffy and ready to be topped with whatever you like the look of. You can choose between their delicious home made sauces (raspberry, salted caramel or chilli chocolate are regular specials) then add toppings (chunks of fresh fruit, or honey roasted pecans, or chopped nuts, or smarties, or marshmallows – you get the picture). Neil brings his skills all the way from New Zealand, Shane comes from Ireland, and like the good boys they are they both cite their mums as their main culinary influence.

RED DOOR CAFÉ

A lovely slice of bohemia halfway down Turnpin Lane, Red Door Café is the perfect spot for when you want to duck out of the bustle of the market. Really popular with the locals, it's furnished with an eclectic mix of furniture, exotic (and slightly mismatched) wallpaper and walls full of paintings and illustrations. On one morning visit there, a dreadlocked harpist was playing almost out of sight behind the tiny bar in exchange for a glass of wine and no-one seemed to bat an eyelid when it transpired that it wasn't a CD. Like being in a charming yet irascible friend's living room – with all their artist pals, terrific coffee and great cakes – it's exactly how a café ought to be.

RETURN TO SHASHAMANE

The most exotically named stall on the market, and one of the most beautiful looking too: Emilia Silvas' Return to Shashamane is a jewelled spread of vegan salads and mezze. Emilia is from Romania and takes a lot of inspiration from vegan Romanian food, but you'll also see plenty of Middle Eastern influences here, too: on any given day you might find tabbouleh with sprouts, basil and pomegranate, for example, or green lentils with mint, peppers, tomatoes and cloves, or red kidney beans with tarragon and cardamom. She uses a lot of herbs and contemporary superfoods as well – expect to taste briny seaweed adding depth to her pulse salads, or fresh turmeric brightening up a bowl of kale and spinach. A real treat, whether you are vegan or not.

RUBYS OF LONDON

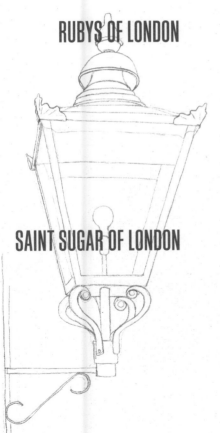

Ruby Amarteifio makes 100 per cent vegan cakes, often gluten- and sugar-free as well. Don't only buy these for what they don't contain though: no matter what your dietary preferences, Ruby's cakes and biscuits are pure pleasure, which must be why they have won at the Baking Industry Awards and have appeared in *Time Out's* 'Best Cakes in London' top ten. She traces her passion for creating vegan 'edible works of art' back to a childhood dairy and egg allergy which left her gazing longingly at other kids' birthday cakes that she couldn't eat. All too often, 'free-from' cakes mean free-from flavour as well – not so with Ruby's peanut butter brownies or her beautiful white chocolate raspberry donuts. Greenwich Market serves as her shop front, but she'll happily deliver a box of her wonderful wares to any address in Greater London.

SAINT SUGAR OF LONDON

Saint Sugar of London are bakers with passion. Owner Enzo Moschetta remembers growing up on a small farm in Italy, and eating his mother's and grandmother's homemade sourdough bread with every meal. Whenever there was any occasion, they would bake special treats, and for him the smell of baking pastries is the smell of childhood – nothing is more evocative. 'Bread is the starting point', he says. 'You cannot have a serious food market without a real bread stall.' Alongside the bread, Saint Sugar sells wonderful pâtisserie: from palmiers, financiers and Florentines to vast pillowy meringues and a range of 'free-from' cakes and biscuits that score high on taste and low on gluten and sugar. Expect a bit of philosophy and learning with your pleasure – Saint Sugar want to remind people how to live and eat well. Their motto? 'Street food = real food for real people.' No shortcuts, no chemicals, no substitutes.

TERIYAKI-YA

Jay Hong is originally from South Korea and is engaging on a not-so-secret mission to popularise some of the flavours from his home country, but his time as head chef of a Japanese restaurant has also been a big influence. One of the first food traders to work in the market, his black-fronted stall mixes up Osakan-style Japanese 'tapas' with south-western Korean cuisine. The stall smells and sounds fantastic as you pass by – the frazzle of frying fish; the sharp sweet tang of his homemade teriyaki sauce – and he serves some of the biggest, freshest tempura prawns you've ever tasted.

THE THAI KITCHEN

Tao, the Thai Kitchen chef, is from north-east Thailand and has been cooking all his life. He grew up surrounded by Thai street foods and when he was eight used to pester the street food vendors on his street until they'd let him help out. As an adult he cooked in hotel restaurants until the idea of the Thai Kitchen took hold and he returned to his first love: street food. Everything is made fresh in small batches, just as it would be in Thailand, and his food sings with fresh herbs and home-ground spice pastes. Tao's other amazing skill is fruit and vegetable carving – he can turn a watermelon into an incredibly intricate bouquet of chrysanthemums, or a pumpkin into a bunch of roses – and sometimes you'll see his work on the stall. Check out his Halloween pumpkin carvings on the Thai Kitchen website!

TORTILLA'S HOME

José is from Malaga and brings a bit of Andalusian charm to the market. He makes juicy, compact individual tortillas in a small cast-iron pan and tops them with a whole host of extras – spicy chorizo burgers, pisto (a delicious slow cooked Spanish ratatouille), pulled lamb, fried eggs – and then rams the whole lot into a freshly baked roll. It's not a light snack but it will keep you going all day and is full of strong, robust flavours. If it's breakfast you're after, do it like a Malagueño and try his fried potatoes and chorizo, topped with a fried egg. Visiting Spaniards are always delighted to find José – you'll not find many better tortillas outside of Spain.

TURNIPS

Caroline and Fred Foster are bona fide market royalty: they've been trading fruit and veg as Turnips for the past twenty years, and three generations of Fosters traded in Pimlico before them. Turnips' truly beautiful stall at Borough Market is a wonder – an astonishing range of fresh produce, opulent piles of florid tomatoes, a bounty of handpicked wild mushrooms. Their outpost at Greenwich focuses less on fresh fruit and veg and more on fantastic coffee and trademark sandwiches and juices that make the most of whatever seasonal produce is available at the time. As Caroline says, 'Our food is mouthwateringly good!' They have great staff in

Greenwich too, always popping between the stalls, calling out to the customers and chatting to the other traders – so why not go in for a chat and one of their enormous cheese toasties.

VEGAN GARDEN

Artist Kaya founded Vegan Garden in 2014 and creates delicious savoury and sweet dishes that look as beautiful as they taste. Everything is baked and cooked daily: rainbow roast vegetables, rich with pumpkin, red onion, carrot and parsley; vegan lasagne laden with tomato and aubergine; individual little spinach and pumpkin quiches sprinkled with pumpkin seeds for goodness and crunch; black forest gateau topped with huge black cherries and dusted with icing sugar or a syrup soaked blueberry drizzle cake – all 100 per cent vegan. Kaya makes the lightest, crumbliest pastry so her tarts and pies are a particular treat.

VICTUS & BIBO

Victus & Bibo was set up in 2005 by husband and wife team Eddie and Fay Aykiran. Their smart black-canopied stall sells 'street food mezze', updating vibrant Turkish flavours with a modern twist, and they have a queue of devoted fans to show for it. Their lamb and halloumi flatbread has special cult status: crumbling lamb mince, heftily seasoned, rolled in a wrap with chargrilled halloumi, red onion, rocket and a pinch of sumac, and juiced up with some tahini and chilli sauce. Make sure you grab a napkin... They also do a terrific *lahmacun*, that under-rated thin Turkish pizza smeared with minced lamb and pomegranate molasses, but be warned – they are always the first thing to sell out so if you fancy one for your lunch, get there early.

MEAT

CHIPOTLE POMEGRANATE CHICKEN QUESADILLAS

❧

MUNCHIES

Quesadillas are basically a delicious snack of melted cheese sandwiched between two tortillas. This is Munchies' take; sweet, smoky chicken quesadillas which they serve on their own, or with tomatillo salsa verde (a green salsa available online from mexgrocer.co.uk) or dipped in hot sauce. Chipotle paste is easy to get hold of in any of the big supermarkets – look for it in the specialist ingredients section. Pomegranate molasses is available in some supermarkets too, but for a more interesting shopping experience go to a Turkish or Middle Eastern deli – you'll definitely find it there amongst all sorts of other delicious things.

Serves 4

- 4 skinless chicken thighs
- 1 teaspoon olive oil
- 2 tablespoons pomegranate molasses
- 45g chipotle paste
- 8 corn or flour tortillas
- 100g Cheddar or Monterey Jack cheese, grated
- seeds from 1 pomegranate
- salt
- freshly ground black pepper

Season each chicken thigh with salt and pepper. Heat a little olive oil in a heavy bottomed pan over a medium heat, and fry the chicken for 5 minutes until golden brown all over. Pour over enough water to just cover the meat and bring to the boil, then turn down the heat and simmer for around 20 minutes. Remove the chicken using tongs or a slotted spoon, and use a couple of forks to shred the meat off the bone (keep the stock to make soup). Mix the shredded chicken with the pomegranate molasses and chipotle paste and a little more salt if you think it needs it.

To make the quesadillas, place one tortilla in a dry frying pan on a low heat. Spoon on a quarter of the shredded chicken mixture, and then scatter with grated cheese and a handful of the pomegranate seed 'jewels'. Place another tortilla on top. Cook the quesadilla for 2 minutes before flipping over and cooking on the other side – if you have any trouble flipping the quesadilla, try using a metal plate or pan lid to turn it over before sliding it back into the pan.

Serve as soon as the outside of the tortilla is golden brown and the fillings are melded together by delicious melted cheese.

CHICKEN KOFTE MEATBALLS

ᔐ

VICTUS & BIBO

Victus & Bibo have one of the most beautiful-smelling stalls at the market, and such is the cult appeal of their food that it always has a huge queue. Their menu is all about traditional Turkish dishes re-jigged and modernised in a street food setting; their robust and zesty flavours are perfectly shown off in these very simple, very delicious meatballs. You can substitute minced lamb for the chicken for a change – just add a little more seasoning.

Serves 4

- 500g minced chicken breast/thigh meat
- 2 red onions, finely chopped
- 4 smallish tomatoes, finely chopped
- 4 garlic cloves, finely chopped
- handful of flat-leaf parsley, finely chopped
- 4 teaspoons red chilli flakes
- 2 teaspoons dried oregano
- 2 teaspoons ground sumac
- 125ml olive oil, plus a little for frying
- salt
- freshly ground black pepper

Put the chicken into a large bowl and add the onions, tomatoes, garlic, parsley, chilli flakes, oregano, sumac, olive oil, 2 teaspoons of salt and 1 teaspoon of black pepper. Knead all the ingredients together to form a smooth paste and then shape the mixture into flattened oval shapes approximately 6cm long and about 2cm thick.

Cover the koftes with clingfilm and put them in the fridge to rest for 15–20 minutes. Then you can either barbecue or pan-fry them in a little olive oil for at least 6–8 minutes, turning once so they are golden brown and crispy on both sides. Be gentle as they are a bit crumbly.

Serve either on a bed of rice with some salad, or in a flatbread with hummus.

THE GREENWICH MARKET COOKBOOK

BÁNH MÌ

❧

BÁNH MÌ NÊN

Vietnamese baguettes, or bánh mì, are one of the happier by-products of a colonial history. The French contributed the baguettes, the mayonnaise and the pâté, and then the Vietnamese made the sandwich their own with a little highly seasoned meat, and lots of the fresh, zesty ingredients that make up the flavours of South East Asia: pickled carrots, chilli, coriander and soy sauce. They are one of Tran's mainstay dishes and a wonderful thing – impossible to eat daintily so don't even try.

Serves 4

- 1 garlic clove, crushed
- 2 shallots, roughly chopped
- 1 teaspoon five-spice powder
- 100ml plus 4 teaspoons soy sauce
- 2 tablespoons honey
- 200g boned skinless chicken thigh or breast
- 4 small white or tiger baguettes
- 100g chicken liver pâté

- 50g mayonnaise (Tran recommends Heinz)
- 1 small cucumber, sliced
- 100g pickled carrots (page 108)
- 1 red onion, finely sliced
- 2 red chillies, finely sliced
- small handful of coriander, roughly chopped
- salt
- freshly ground black pepper

First make the marinade for the chicken. Put the garlic, shallots, five-spice powder, 100ml of the soy sauce and the honey in a blender with plenty of black pepper and blitz until smooth. Pour over the chicken and put in the fridge for at least an hour or, ideally, overnight to let the flavours kick in.

Preheat the oven to 180ºC. Put the chicken, in its marinade, in an ovenproof dish. Bake for 30 minutes, leave to cool slightly, then slice or shred the meat depending on how you like it. You could also barbecue the marinated chicken instead of baking it for an amazing smoky flavour.

Put the baguettes into the oven for 5 minutes to get hot and crispy. Then, quickly, cut each one in half lengthwise and pull out some of the soft white bread inside so you can fit more filling in. Spread one half with chicken liver pâté and the other with mayonnaise. Then build your baguette with some chicken, a few slices of cucumber, some pickled carrots, a few slices of red onion, and red chilli and coriander to taste. Season with salt and a little black pepper, then sprinkle each sandwich with a teaspoon of soy sauce.

VIETNAMESE PANCAKES

❧

BÁNH MÌ NÊN

This is a great starter or light lunch – a thin, crispy coconut pancake stuffed with chicken, prawns and beansprouts and served with fresh coriander, mint and a salty-sour dipping sauce. It's a very straightforward batter but you really do need a non-stick frying pan to cook it. The key is to let the pan get really hot, then turn the heat down to low when you start frying the pancake.

Serves 4

for the batter:
- 150g rice flour
- 270ml coconut milk
- ½ teaspoon turmeric powder
- ¼ teaspoon salt

for the dipping sauce:
- 2 tablespoons sugar
- 2 tablespoons fish sauce
- 1 tablespoon freshly squeezed lime juice
- 1 garlic clove, crushed
- 1–2 chillies, finely chopped

for the stuffing:
- 100g chicken fillets, thinly sliced
- 100g raw prawns, shelled
- 1 small onion, sliced
- 100g beansprouts
- 100g mushrooms, sliced
- bunch of spring onions, chopped
- 4 teaspoons olive oil
- ½ iceberg lettuce, shredded
- small handful of mint
- small handful of coriander
- salt
- freshly ground black pepper

First make the batter. Mix the rice flour, coconut milk, turmeric and salt together in a big bowl and leave to rest in the fridge for 30 minutes. If it looks too thick, add another 30ml coconut milk or water so you have the consistency of double cream.

Make the dipping sauce: add the sugar, fish sauce, lime juice, garlic and chillies to 250ml water and stir until the sugar has dissolved.

Put the chicken in one bowl and the prawns in another and season both with salt and pepper.

When you're ready to eat, put a teaspoon of olive oil in small non-stick frying pan on a medium-high heat. Once it's good and hot, add about a quarter of the onion and fry for a minute. Next, add a quarter of the chicken and prawns and fry briefly until the chicken is pale and the prawns have turned pink. Turn the heat down to low. Ladle over enough batter to thinly cover the base of the pan – tip the pan around so it spreads evenly and is as thin as possible. Scatter a handful each of beansprouts, mushrooms and spring onions over one half of the pancake, then cover and leave to cook for 3 minutes. When the batter is cooked through and crispy on the bottom and edges, fold over the side with no filling on it to form a half moon. Cut into four pieces and serve hot on a bed of iceberg lettuce, coriander and mint with the dipping sauce on the side. Repeat with the remaining ingredients to make three more pancakes. Each diner can then roll up bits of pancake with the cool crisp shreds of lettuce and herbs inside, and dip it into the sauce before eating.

CHICKEN AND CASHEW NUT STIR-FRY

❧

THAI KITCHEN

This one's super tasty and super quick – like all stir-fries, the only thing that takes more than a moment is the prep. So get your ingredients sliced up ready to go and you'll have dinner on the table in 10 minutes tops.

Serves 4

- 1 tablespoon olive oil
- 3 garlic cloves, finely chopped
- 750g chicken breast, sliced across into 1cm strips
- 2 teaspoons oyster sauce
- 2 teaspoons soy sauce
- 1 teaspoon chicken stock powder (or ½ chicken stock cube)
- 2 teaspoons sugar

- 1 red pepper, halved and sliced lengthwise
- 1 green pepper, halved sliced lengthwise
- 1 onion, halved and thinly sliced
- 2 carrots, halved and sliced lengthwise
- 150g unsalted roasted cashew nuts
- bunch of spring onions, cut into 3cm lengths

Put the oil in a large non-stick frying pan or wok over a medium-high heat. When it's good and hot, add the garlic and stir for 30 seconds until fragrant, then throw in the chicken. Stir-fry until the chicken is just cooked through – 5 minutes or so – then quickly add the oyster sauce, soy sauce, chicken stock powder and sugar. Give it a stir to mix, then add the sliced peppers, onion and carrots and cook for another 2–4 minutes until the vegetables are just starting to soften. Finally, put the cashew nuts and spring onions into the pan, cook for just long enough to heat them through and then serve.

RICE NOODLES WITH HONEY LEMONGRASS CHICKEN

✺

BÁNH MÌ NÊN

This is another lovely meal from Tran at Bánh Mì Nên , like a summer party in a bowl. It's full of fresh, colourful ingredients – crisp salad and herbs, slippy cool rice noodles, flavour-packed chicken, a bit of crunch and salt from the peanuts. Fab.

Serves 4

- 2 garlic cloves, crushed
- 1 shallot, chopped
- 50ml soy sauce
- 2 tablespoons honey
- 50g lemongrass, finely chopped
- 1kg boneless chicken thighs or breasts
- 600g 1.2mm rice noodles
- 1 iceberg lettuce or bag of mixed salad
- small handful of coriander
- small handful of mint

- 1 red onion, thinly sliced
- 1 small cucumber, thinly sliced
- 50g beansprouts
- pickled carrots (page 108)
- 60g roasted salted peanuts, roughly chopped

for the dipping sauce:
- 2 tablespoons fish sauce
- 1 tablespoon freshly squeezed lime juice or rice vinegar
- 2 tablespoons sugar
- ¼ garlic clove, crushed
- 1–2 chillies, finely chopped

First marinate your chicken. Put the garlic, shallot, soy sauce and honey in a blender and blitz until you have a smooth sauce – a stick blender will do this in moments. Add the lemongrass, and pour the mixture over the chicken pieces. Leave for at least an hour in the fridge – or even better, overnight. When you're ready to cook, transfer the whole lot to an ovenproof dish and cook in the oven at 180°C for 40 minutes. When the chicken is cooked, take the pieces out of the sauce and slice or shred the meat. Mix with a couple of tablespoons of the cooking sauce and put to one side.

Next, make the dipping sauce. In a small bowl mix the fish sauce, lime juice and sugar with 250ml hot water and stir to dissolve the sugar. Taste – if it's too salty or sour for you, add another 50ml water. When it's cooled down, stir in the garlic and chillies.

Bring 2 litres of water to the boil, then put in the rice noodles and boil for 5–8 minutes until they are just al dente. Keep an eye on them as they can overcook really easily. Drain them well and rinse with cool water, then leave them aside in a colander. Shred the iceberg lettuce if that's what you're using, and roughly chop the herbs.

To serve, divide the rice noodles and the cooked chicken between four big bowls. Add a handful of the iceberg lettuce or mixed salad, some coriander and mint, a few slices of red onion and cucumber, a handful of beansprouts and some pickled carrots. Sprinkle some peanuts over each bowlful, and hand to your expectant, hungry guests with a small bowl (50ml or so per person) of the dipping sauce. They can then pour it over and stir everything together before digging in.

TRADITIONAL PHO NOODLE SOUP

~

BÁNH MÌ NÊN

The easiest way to make this is to buy a whole chicken and cut off the breast and thigh meat before you cook it, then use the carcass to make the broth. You get an aromatic, deep amber-coloured liquid, which smells and tastes wonderful. The recipe uses crystalline rock sugar as this doesn't cloud the broth – it is easily available in any Chinese supermarket but if you can't find it, just use caster sugar instead.

This recipe makes a lot of broth, so it's worth freezing any leftovers and you'll be able to cobble together a nearly instant pho at any time.

Serves 4

- 400g 5mm rice noodles
- 1 chicken
- 3 onions
  (2 left whole, 1 finely sliced)
- 5 shallots
- 5 thin slices fresh ginger
- 25g rock sugar
- 1 cinnamon stick
- 5 star anise
- 1 tablespoon coriander seeds
- 2 cardamom seeds
- 10 cloves
- 4 spring onions, finely sliced
- small bunch of coriander, roughly chopped
- 100g beansprouts
- 4 limes, quartered
- 4 birds-eye chillies, finely chopped
- small bunch of of mint, roughly chopped
- salt

Put the dried noodles in a bowl of cold water to soften.

With a large, sharp knife, remove the breast and thigh fillets from the chicken. Chop off the drumsticks and save them for another recipe. Bring a large pan of water to the boil, then add the chicken carcass and breast and thigh fillets and boil gently for 5 minutes. Drain in a colander and rinse in cold water.

Bring 3.5 litres of water to the boil, then add the carcass and fillets, the two whole onions, the shallots (again, left whole), the ginger, rock sugar and a tablespoon of salt. Bring to the boil again, then turn the heat down to low and simmer very gently for 30 minutes. Don't cover it with a lid, and keep skimming off any fat that forms on the surface to get a beautiful clear broth. Remove the breast and thigh fillets with a slotted spoon and put them to one side, then slice them when they've cooled down a bit.

Simmer the broth for another 30 minutes, then carefully strain into a large bowl, and pour it back into the pan. Make a spice bag (a clean pop sock is useful here, or tie up a small square of muslin) with the cinnamon, star anise, coriander seeds, cardamom and cloves and pop it into the pan, then simmer for another 15 minutes. Meanwhile, slice the poached chicken fillets.

When it's time to eat, drain the noodles and heat them up. A microwave is easiest: just put the noodles in a large bowl, cover with fresh water and microwave on high for 2 minutes. If you don't have a microwave, pour boiling water over the softened noodles and leave them for 7 minutes or so until al dente, then drain and refresh under cold water.

Line up four large soup bowls ready to serve. In each one, put a quarter of the cooked noodles, then add some chicken, onion, spring onion and coriander. Ladle over about 350ml of the golden stock per serving, and serve with separate plates of beansprouts, quartered limes, chillies and chopped mint for people to add as they like.

SLOW-COOKED CHICKEN WITH LEMONGRASS

≈

BÁNH MÌ NÊN

This is a very simple, soothing recipe. It makes a perfect lunch or dinner and is just the sort of thing you might want to eat if you're out of sorts bodily or mentally. The coconut water is a great touch – imparting a very subtle sweetness and coconut flavour without any of the heaviness of coconut milk. The lemongrass lends zest and vigour, but not overpoweringly so. Tran suggests adding some sliced red chilli with the vegetables at the end if you want some heat – it's really very good either way.

Serves 4

- 500g chicken breast fillets
- 1 tablespoon olive oil
- 2 shallots, finely chopped
- 2 garlic cloves, finely chopped
- 500ml coconut water
- 1 chicken stock cube
- 2 stalks of lemongrass
- 1 small carrot, diced
- 1 potato, diced
- 25g mushrooms, sliced
- 1 small onion, halved and sliced
- salt
- freshly ground black pepper

Cut the chicken into 2cm cubes and season with a little salt and black pepper. In a large pot or wok, heat the olive oil over a medium heat and then cook the shallots and garlic for a minute. Add the chicken and fry, stirring to stop it sticking, for 5 minutes. Pour in the coconut water, then crumble in the stock cube and add half a teaspoon of salt. Chop the lemongrass into 2cm lengths and crush it lightly with the back of your knife, then add to the pot and bring everything to the boil. Turn the heat down to low and simmer for 40 minutes, uncovered.

Add the carrot, potato, mushrooms and onion to the pot. Simmer for another 15 minutes or until the vegetables are tender. Check for seasoning, then serve hot with steamed rice or rice noodles.

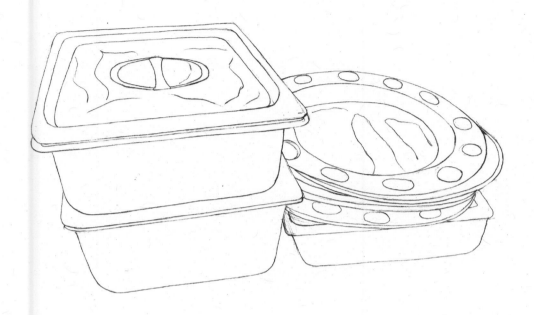

"WE'VE BEEN HERE NEARLY SEVEN YEARS. WHAT KEEPS US HERE IS THE BEAUTY OF THE SETTING AND ALL OUR REGULAR CUSTOMERS – THAI PEOPLE TRAVEL FROM AROUND LONDON TO EAT THE FOOD THAT TAO, OUR CHEF, COOKS. OUR MOST POPULAR DISHES ARE HIS SPICY BEEF OR VEGETABLE PAD THAI WITH TOFU. AND EVERYONE LOVES GREEN CURRY." Martin, *Thai Kitchen*

CHICKEN THAI GREEN CURRY

~~

THAI KITCHEN

Tao and Martin bring their Thai Kitchen to the market every weekend and this classic green curry is always a sell-out dish for them. Hot, sweet, sharp and zesty all at once, it's delicious with a cold beer and is easy and quick to make.

Serves 4

- 2 teaspoons olive oil
- 75g green curry paste
- 2 × 400ml tins coconut milk
- 3 lime leaves,
  each torn into 3 pieces
- 750g chicken breast, sliced across
  into 1cm strips
- 300g courgettes, diced
- 2–3 teaspoons sugar
- 3 teaspoons fish sauce
- 50g Thai basil leaves
  (reserve 12 leaves for the garnish)

Put the olive oil in a large wok or non-stick frying pan over a medium heat, then add the curry paste and fry for a minute or so until fragrant. Add the coconut milk and lime leaves and bring to the boil, then stir in the chicken and turn down to a simmer.

After about 5 minutes, add the courgettes and simmer for 10 minutes longer until the chicken is cooked and the courgettes are just tender. Stir in the sugar to taste along with the fish sauce, then finally rip the Thai basil leaves into the curry. Serve immediately in bowls, each one garnished with 3 whole basil leaves.

NILGIRI MURGH

~

MOGUL

This may well become your go-to chicken curry recipe. The nilgiri masala that forms its base is an absolute cinch to make and infuses the chicken with the mild, sweet fresh flavours of mint, coriander and coconut. It keeps well in the fridge for a week, so keep any left over from this recipe – it works well as a marinade for grilled or roast chicken as an alternative to curry. It's also a dish that's really popular with children – though if you are making if for kids you might want to leave out or cut down on the chilli powder.

Serves 2

for the nilgiri masala:
- 2 teaspoons sunflower oil
- 1 teaspoons coriander seeds
- ¾ teaspoon cumin seeds
- ¾ teaspoon fennel seeds
- 1 star anise
- 10 cashew nuts (unsalted)
- 2 green cardamom pods
- 3 cloves
- 1 cinnamon stick
- 90g grated coconut (fresh or desiccated)
- 10–12 curry leaves
- 1 tablespoon chopped coriander
- 15–18 mint leaves

for the curry:
- 1½ tablespoons sunflower oil
- 2 onions, finely chopped
- 2 teaspoons ginger and garlic paste
- 1 tomato, finely chopped
- 1 teaspoon red chilli powder
- ¾ teaspoon turmeric
- 500g boneless chicken breast or thigh, diced
- 1 teaspoon freshly squeezed lemon juice
- chopped coriander, for garnish
- salt

First make the nilgiri masala. Heat the sunflower oil in a frying pan over a low heat and then add all the spices from the coriander seeds down to the cinnamon stick. Fry gently for 2 minutes, then stir in the coconut and curry leaves and fry for another 3 minutes. Using a blender or a food processor, grind the mixture to a smooth paste with 250ml water. Add the fresh coriander and mint and process again, then set aside.

Now get on with the curry itself. Heat the oil in a large pan over a medium heat. Add the onion and fry for 5 minutes or so until golden brown. Add the ginger and garlic paste, tomato, chilli powder and turmeric and cook for 2–3 minutes. When the tomato has cooked down a little, stir in a generous tablespoon and a half of your nilgiri masala along with 50ml water, and stir-fry for 2 minutes. Add the chicken and some salt, mix it well with the masala, and keep stirring for 5 minutes. Add 250ml water, then reduce the heat and simmer until the chicken is fully cooked. Stir in the lemon juice and chilli powder and check the seasoning, adding more salt to taste.

Garnish with some more chopped coriander leaves and serve with roti and steamed basmati rice.

STEWED CHICKEN

∽

ARAWAK GRILL

This is real Jamaican home-style cooking from the Arawak Grill crew, and makes a super tasty and super straight-forward dinner. It's worth jointing a chicken for – just chop each portion into two or three pieces once you're done – but you could use the equivalent weight of drumsticks and thighs, each cut into two.

Serves 4–6

- 1 whole chicken (about 1.2kg), chopped into 18–20 pieces
- 1 onion, roughly chopped
- 1 Scotch bonnet, (deseeded if you like) and finely chopped
- 1 sweet red pepper, roughly chopped
- 3 tomatoes, roughly chopped
- 3 spring onions, chopped
- 3 garlic cloves, chopped
- 1.5cm piece fresh ginger, finely chopped
- 1 chicken stock cube
- 1 teaspoon gravy browning
- salt
- freshly ground black pepper

Put a large pot over a high heat. When the pot begins to smoke, bang in the chicken pieces and season with about a teaspoon of salt and black pepper. There is no need for any oil as the skin and fat will break down and give you all the oil you need, but be sure to keep stirring and shaking the pot to stop it sticking. Once the chicken pieces have started to brown all over, add the onion, Scotch bonnet, red pepper, tomatoes, spring onions, garlic and ginger and keep frying and stirring until they soften. Pour in 1 litre of water, add the chicken stock cube and gravy browning, then lower the heat and simmer for 45 minutes.

Serve hot with some plain steamed rice or rice and peas – however you like.

GUAVA BBQ TOSTADA MOUNTAIN

❧

MUNCHIES

This is one of those fantastic build-your-own dinners that's great when you have a crowd to feed. While there's a bit of prep to do, it's not very difficult – you need five hours to leave the pork to cook, but everything else you can throw together in the last hour while drinking a cold beer. Put it all out on the table and let people experiment with the different toppings and build up their own tostada mountains as high as they like.

You can make mini blue, gluten-free, fried tortillas yourself: it's very easy. Maseca azul, made from a special variety of blue corn, is available from a website called mexgrocer.co.uk (and also from other Mexican and Latin American importers and whole food shops), and tends to be more robust than its yellow and white counterparts. If you really don't have time, buy small corn tortillas and fry them.

Serves 8

for the pork:
- 1 small pork shoulder (about 1.2kg)
- smoked paprika
- 150–300ml guava juice
- 200ml BBQ sauce (page 106)
- salt

for the salsa:
- 6 plum tomatoes, roughly chopped
- ½ red onion, roughly chopped
- small bunch of coriander, roughly chopped
- ½ Scotch bonnet chilli (use habanero if available), roughly chopped
- juice of ½ lime

for the toppings:
- ½ small fresh red cabbage (or pickled if you prefer)
- juice of ½ lime
- ½ teaspoon sugar
- 200g Cheddar cheese, grated
- 200g tinned black beans, drained
- ½ teaspoon dried oregano (Mexican if available)
- fresh guava, radishes or avocado to garnish

for the tostadas:
- 200g Maseca azul
- pinch of salt
- sunflower oil, for deep frying

First make the pulled pork, remembering you will need 5 hours! Preheat the oven to its highest heat. Score the skin of the pork shoulder with a very sharp knife and rub with a little salt and smoked paprika. Put it in a roasting dish in the middle of the oven and immediately turn the heat down to 160ºC. Leave for 2 hours before turning the oven down to 150ºC for another 2 hours. For the final hour, turn the oven down to 100ºC, occasionally basting the skin of the pork in its own juices.

During the final hour of cooking the pork, prepare all the other components of your tostada mountain. To make the salsa, whizz together the tomatoes, onion, coriander, chilli and lime juice and put in a small bowl. Very finely chop the red cabbage and dress with lime juice and a little sugar. Put the grated cheese in a bowl. Gently warm up the black beans in a small pan, and season with a sprinkling of salt and Mexican oregano. Finally, prepare whatever garnish you are using: grate the fresh guava, chop up the avocado into small cubes or thinly slice the radish.

When the pork is cooked, take it out of the oven and leave it to cool down a bit, then remove the crackling and either discard it (are you crazy?) or break it off in pieces and dip in guacamole for a cook's treat. While the pork is still warm, shred with two forks – it will fall apart nice and easily. Drain off any cooking liquid and put the shredded meat into a bowl. Mix in the guava juice and BBQ sauce – guava juice can be very sweet so use 150ml to begin with and add more according to taste. Season with a bit of salt.

The very last thing to do is make the tostadas. They need to be served hot and crispy, fresh from the frying pan, so make them immediately after you've mixed the guava juice and BBQ sauce into the pork so that everything can be served as freshly cooked as possible. Heat up 3cm of sunflower oil in a frying pan. While it's getting hot, put the Maseca into a bowl with a pinch of salt and add 250ml water little by little, mixing as you go along until you have a doughy consistency that holds together.

With your hands, roll the dough into small balls about the size of a conker – Munchies make about eight per person. Flatten each one in your palm with the heel of the other hand to make a tortilla about 8cm across and drop into the hot oil for 30 seconds to 1 minute on each side. It's really obvious when they're done – the tostadas will crisp and darken to a deep purple brown.

Hand out the hot tostadas on serving plates and everyone can start to construct their mountains from the toppings you have prepared. First put on some grated cheese (so that it melts a bit), then a handful of cabbage, then some juicy pork, then the salsa. Spoon over some black beans, then sprinkle on your guava/avocado/radish garnish and maybe a bit more cheese for luck. Enjoy!

PAN ABIERTO DE SOBRASADA Y MURCIA AL VINO

∽

HOLA PAELLA

Hola Paella sells a whole range of Spanish meats and cheeses, and this grilled open sandwich features two of the finest. Sobrasada is a kind of spreadable chorizo from the Balearic islands – soft, oily, slightly spicy. Murcia al vino is a semi-hard goat's cheese that is cured in red wine to give it a distinctive purple skin. While both are delicious enough on their own, they grill up beautifully together here, the sobrasada releasing some of its deep orange oil into the bread, the cheese blistering under the heat.

Serves 4

- 1 small baguette
- 300g sobrasada señorio Ibérico
- 200g Murcia al vino cheese
- 4 teaspoons lavender honey
- handful of rocket leaves
- olive oil
- freshly ground black pepper

Set the grill to high. Cut the baguette in half and then slice each piece lengthwise. Spread the baguette slices generously with the sobrasada. Slice the Murcia al vino into thin triangles, and arrange on top of the sobrasada in overlapping arrows. Put the open sandwiches under the hot grill until the cheese melts and starts to bubble. Remove to a plate and drizzle a teaspoon of lavender honey over each one, followed by a good grind of black pepper. Serve with the rocket on the side, simply dressed with a slug of good-quality olive oil.

BBQ PULLED PORK

৵৽

NO. 57A

No. 57A's artisan flatbreads are a staple of the food market: lovely and soft, with slightly blistered outsides and a fluffy crumb inside. The recipe is, unsurprisingly, a closely guarded secret but Marzia and Matteo didn't mind sharing with us some of their wonderful fillings. Their BBQ Pulled Pork is a winner, especially when stuffed into a flatbread with melted cheese, homemade coleslaw and a sprinkling of chives on top. It's also good with salad and some gherkins on the side.

Serves 4

- 1kg pork shoulder, skinned and boned
- 1 tablespoon dark brown sugar
- 1 tablespoon salt
- ½ teaspoon ground cumin
- ¼ teaspoon ground cinnamon
- 1 white onion, sliced
- 1 garlic clove, finely chopped
- BBQ sauce (page 106)

Preheat the oven to 170ºC.

Cut the pork shoulder into three or four big pieces and trim any excess fat and skin, then pat dry with a towel. Mix the sugar, salt, cumin and cinnamon in a small bowl then rub it evenly all over the meat. Put the pork in a high-sided roasting tin and add the onions and garlic. Pour in 250ml water, cover tightly with foil and put in the oven to roast for 7 hours.

When the pork is cooked, take the pieces of meat out of the cooking liquid and scrape off any onions or garlic. Using two forks, shred the meat into small pieces. Serve in flatbreads or floury baps, drizzled with as much BBQ sauce as you like.

BBQ PORK BELLY

❧

PIG DOGS AND BRISKET

Imagine BBQ ribs, and then imagine them double their normal size and covered in the best BBQ sauce you'll ever eat. Then remember to search out Kelvin at the Pig Dogs and Brisket van and thank him for the recipe.

Serves 4

• 2kg skinless pork belly with ribs attached

• 70g BBQ rub (page 105)
• 200ml BBQ sauce (page 106)

Rub the pork belly all over with the BBQ rub and place in the fridge for at least 2 hours or better still, overnight.

Preheat the oven to 150ºC. Put the pork belly on a rack in a deep roasting tray with 1cm water in the bottom. Cover the whole thing tightly with foil and cook in the oven for 2 hours. Remove the foil and roast for a further hour. Remove the meat from the oven and allow to cool – if you can, leave it overnight.

Cut the pork belly into thick slices with the rib bone attached and put them on a baking tray, then pour over some of the BBQ sauce. Put the ribs under a hot grill for 5–10 minutes, then turn them over and apply more BBQ sauce – keep turning and basting until the ribs are glazed with all the sauce.

Serve with Pickled Watermelon (page 107) and Macaroni Cheese (page 79).

PORK BELLY WITH CHILLI PEPPERS

❧

GOOD FORTUNE CHINESE FOOD

David is originally from Liaoning Province in north-eastern China, but he loves to cook food from Hunan in the south where they like to eat with a lot of heat. In Hunan, this home-style and delicious pork belly stir-fry would be cooked with a very hot green chilli that he's never been able to find here. Instead he uses Sivri peppers – those long, pale green sabre-shaped ones from Turkey. They are not particularly spicy so if you want to up the heat just add a few chopped birds-eye chillies. This is a fantastically tasty and super quick dish – 10 minutes from start to finish. You do, however, need really thin slices of pork belly around 2mm thick – the easiest way to do this is to put the meat in the freezer for 30 minutes until it is slightly frozen before you slice it.

Serves 4

• 2 tablespoons sunflower oil
• 300g skinless pork belly, very thinly sliced
• 2 tablespoons light soy sauce
• 1 tablespoon dark soy sauce
• 1 tablespoon rice vinegar
• 250g long green peppers, sliced

Heat the oil in a big wok over a medium heat and add the pork (be careful, the oil will splatter). Turn up the heat to high and stir-fry briskly, until every piece of meat has just lost its pink colour. Add the light soy sauce, the dark soy sauce and the vinegar, then throw in the peppers. Stir-fry for another 1–2 minutes until the peppers have softened and their skins have started to pucker.

Serve with rice and cabbage fried with soy sauce and a chopped clove of garlic.

CASSAVA LEAVES WITH PORK AND RICE

(Ravitoto sy Henakisoa ary vary)

LE LEMURIEN

Lilia gave us this recipe as, to her, it is the taste of home cooking in Madagascar. Ravitoto is not something you really get in restaurants, more something that your mother has cooked for you since you were small, a dish that will be made differently in every Malagasy household. Lilia doesn't actually serve it at her stall but she says her British husband has come to love it more, even, than her fantastic coconut chicken. It is an acquired taste and texture: earthy, almost grassy, with a slightly sharp, acidic taste that cuts perfectly through the bland fattiness of the pork belly. Cassava leaves need to be pounded to remove all traces of the naturally occurring cyanide – if you're lucky and live near an African market, you may be able to find it freshly pounded, but it's more likely you'll find it in the freezer section of an African grocer under the name of Pondu. Let it defrost thoroughly before you start cooking.

Serves 4

- 3 tablespoons oil
- 800g skinless pork belly, roughly chopped
- 7 garlic cloves, finely chopped
- 400g pounded cassava leaves (frozen or fresh)
- 1 teaspoon sugar (optional)
- salt

Heat 1½ tablespoons of oil in a large frying pan until it's good and hot. Add the pork belly and cook over a medium heat until it is brown all over. Season well, then add 125ml water and leave it to simmer until the liquid has cooked off – about 10 minutes.

In another pan, add the remaining oil and the garlic. Fry until it's just golden, then stir in the cassava leaves. Keep stirring over a medium low heat as they soften and become a darker green, then add the cooked pork belly and mix it in well. Sprinkle over the sugar if you're using it and taste for seasoning. Add another 180ml water then turn the heat right down and simmer, covered, until there is very little liquid left in the pan.

Serve over white rice, and dream of the jungles and beaches of Madagascar.

CURRY GOAT

❧

ARAWAK GRILL

Curry goat is one of the most famous of all Jamaican staples, and Arawak Grill's chef Robert cooks a legendary version. Robert says, 'Whenever there is an excuse for a get-together in Jamaica, we'll get started ('run a boat') on the curry goat. Most people cook it outdoors on a coal stove, and once done – you'd better get your helping quickly!' If you can't get goat, use lamb, and give the dish plenty of time to simmer away as that's what gets the meat so tender. Either way, get your butcher to chop it on the bone for full flavour.

Serves 4

- 1kg goat or lamb, cut into 5cm pieces
- 5 tablespoons curry powder (Betapak curry powder for the authentic Jamaican taste)
- 2 hot chillies (ideally Scotch bonnet), finely chopped
- 1 tablespoon grated fresh ginger
- 6 garlic cloves, finely chopped
- 2 sprigs thyme
- ½ teaspoon salt
- ½ teaspoon freshly ground black pepper
- 1 tablespoon butter
- 1 tablespoon sunflower oil
- 2 onions, diced
- 200g carrots, diced
- 200g potatoes, peeled and diced

Put the meat into a large bowl, then add the curry powder, chillies, ginger, garlic, thyme, salt and black pepper. Massage the spices thoroughly into the meat and then put in the fridge for at least 20 minutes to let the flavours mingle and develop.

Put the butter and oil in a saucepan or casserole large enough to take all the meat, and put over a medium heat. When the butter has melted, brown the meat in batches, then return it all to the pan with the onions and cook until the onions are soft and translucent. Stir in the carrots and potatoes, then pour in enough water to just cover the meat. Make sure you scrape all the wonderful flavours up from the bottom of the pan. Bring to the boil then simmer very slowly for about 1½ hours, until the meat is tender and falling off the bone.

Serve with plain white rice and a fresh salad and like Robert says, get in there quickly as it won't be around for long.

RAMEN BURGERS

❧

PIMP MY RAMEN

Harry of Pimp My Ramen is, quite rightly, increasingly famous for these delicious and eccentric burgers. Instead of buns, he fries up patties of pressed ramen noodles which are golden and crispy on the outside, and soft and noodly on the inside. Put a simple burger made out of really good steak mince in the middle, add some melted cheese and a fried egg and you have a huge and very tasty lunch. The Ramen Burger is also impossible to eat without getting it all over your face so you might as well give into it.

Season the ramen 'bun' with whatever spice mix you like: try a jerk seasoning mix or a BBQ spice rub (like Pig Dogs and Brisket's on p105).

Serves 2

- 100g dried ramen noodles
- 3 large eggs
- ½–1 teaspoon spice mix (BBQ, jerk, five-spice – whatever you like)
- 250g beef steak mince
- 50g mature Cheddar or Edam cheese, sliced
- 1½ teaspoons sunflower oil
- rocket or shredded lettuce
- ketchup, mayo or sweet chilli sauce
- salt
- freshly ground black pepper

Cook the noodles in boiling water according to the instructions on the packet until just tender, then drain them in a colander and refresh with cold water. Let them drain for a couple of minutes. Beat one of the eggs in a large bowl, then add the noodles and whatever seasoning you are using. Mix well. Lightly grease four ramekins about the size of a burger bun, and divide the noodles between them. Pack them down tightly, put something heavy on top (a tin of beans wrapped in foil works well) and refrigerate for at least an hour.

When you're ready to eat, season the steak mince with salt and pepper and shape it into two burgers a little larger than the noodle ramekins (they will shrink while cooking). Fry the burgers on a lightly greased hot griddle for 3–5 minutes on each side depending on how rare you like them. Once you've turned them, top the cooked side with the sliced cheese, which will slowly melt as the burger cooks.

Put a teaspoon of sunflower oil into a large frying pan over a medium heat. When it's good and hot, carefully turn out the noodle 'buns' into the pan and fry for 2 minutes on each side until they are golden brown and crispy. Fry the remaining two eggs until cooked but still runny in the middle.

Now assemble your Ramen Burger! Put one of the noodle buns on a plate, and lay some rocket or shredded lettuce on top. Put on a burger, add a squirt of ketchup, mayo or sweet chilli sauce, then put a fried egg on top of that. Finish off with the other noodle bun and apply to your face.

MEATBALLS IN TOMATO SAUCE

NO. 57A

These are great served on their own, with toasted bread or, as Marzia and Matteo like it, in homemade flatbreads. Or you could even have them with pasta but, as Marzia says, 'We know this may sound shocking but spaghetti and meatballs is not an Italian dish... But if you like it, go for it!'

Serves 4

- 600g minced beef
- big handful of parsley, finely chopped
- 1 egg
- 2 tablespoons plain flour
- 2 tablespoons extra virgin olive oil
- 2 garlic cloves, finely chopped
- 600g Italian tomato passata
- pinch of sugar
- bunch of basil
- salt
- freshly ground black pepper

Place the minced beef, parsley and egg in a large mixing bowl. Add the flour and a generous pinch of salt and black pepper and mix all the ingredients together thoroughly. Wet your hands and shape the mixture into balls the size of an apricot – you should get around 20.

Heat a tablespoon of the olive oil in a large saucepan, then add the garlic and cook until it is sizzling and golden. Then add the passata with a pinch of sugar and salt and black pepper to taste, and cover. Let it simmer for 20 minutes or so. Start cooking the meatballs separately to stop them from breaking up: put the remaining olive oil in a wide frying pan over a medium heat. Add the meatballs (in batches if necessary) and fry until they are firm and golden brown all over.

Once the meatballs are cooked, put them gently in the sauce, shaking the pan to make sure they are all well covered, and simmer with the lid on for another 15 minutes. Just before you eat, tear in the basil leaves and enjoy.

BURRITO PABELLON

(Venezuelan Burrito)

∼⌣∼

MUNCHIES

Pabellon is a dish eaten in a few different Latin American countries (including Venezuela, where Munchies' very own Emmanuel hails from) consisting of slow cooked shredded beef, rice, black beans, avocado and plantain. This is one of the star dishes at their Greenwich stall: they serve the pabellon inside a burrito so that folk can walk around the market while enjoying it. It is perfect street food! Make sure you take advantage of their truly incredibly selection of hot sauces while you're there – some do actually make your eyes water, but they have some gentler ones on offer too.

Serves 4–6

For the beef
- 500g topside beef,
  cut into 4cm pieces
- 2 small onions, finely sliced
- 2 small green peppers,
  roughly chopped
- 2 beef tomatoes,
  roughly chopped
- 2 tablespoons tomato puree
- 3 teaspoons cumin powder
- 4 teaspoons capers
- splash of vinegar
- splash of olive oil
- handful of coriander, chopped
- salt

For the burritos
- 200g white rice
- 1 teaspoon cumin seeds
- 2 teaspoon olive oil
- 400g tin black beans, drained
- 1 teaspoon dried oregano
  (Mexican if available)
- 1 large plantain
- 4 large corn or flour tortillas
- 1 lettuce, shredded
- 100g salty white cheese, crumbled
- 1 avocado, thinly sliced
- hot sauce (optional)

You'll need to start on the beef well in advance. Put the beef, onions, green peppers, tomatoes, tomato puree, cumin, capers, vinegar and olive oil in a large saucepan. Add the chopped coriander and a pinch of salt, then pour in 200ml of water. Bring to the boil, then immediately turn down the heat and simmer for 6 hours, stirring occasionally to make sure nothing sticks to the bottom of the pan. Once cooked, the meat will be rich in taste and should fall apart easily. Drain any liquid from the pan, then shred the beef with two forks.

When the beef is nearly done, get on with the other burrito fillings. Cook the rice in salted water. While it is cooking, gently toast the cumin seeds in a teaspoon of olive oil in a small frying pan, then stir them into the cooked and drained rice. Gently warm the black beans along with some Mexican oregano and a pinch of salt. Peel the plantain, and cut into four lengthwise. Fry the strips in a teaspoon of olive oil until they are golden brown.

Set your grill to its highest setting. Lay out the tortillas and put all of the fillings in a line along the centre, being careful not to overfill as this will make them difficult to roll. As a rule of thumb, cover no more than a third of the surface of the tortilla. Hungry Payaso usually put the following in each one: 3 tablespoons of rice, a small handful of lettuce, 4 tablespoons of shredded beef, a small handful of crumbled cheese, a tablespoon of black beans, three slices of avocado, one strip of plantain, and a few drops of hot sauce (*Valentina Muy Picante* is their favourite). Now roll your burrito. Assuming the line of ingredients goes from left to right, fold over the left and right edges of the tortilla towards the centre. Pick up the edge closest to you, and tuck it over the filling, then roll up as tightly as possible so you have a neat little package with no filling leaking out.

Put the burritos on a baking tray under the grill for 6–7 minutes, then serve. If you want to eat them on the go, wrap them in foil to prevent them from falling apart as you eat them.

SPICY BEEF STIR-FRY

❧

THAI KITCHEN

Another cracker from the boys at Thai Kitchen – simple and hot and packed full of flavour. Once you've got everything sliced, it only takes minutes to cook up – tender steak, crunchy beans and peppers vibrant with colour and the peppery punch of Thai basil bringing it all together.

Serves 4

• 4–5 red birds-eye chillies
• 2–3 garlic cloves
• 2 teaspoons olive oil
• 750g rump steak, sliced into finger-sized strips
• 2 teaspoons oyster sauce
• 2 teaspoons soy sauce
• 1 beef stock cube
• 2 teaspoons sugar
• 300g green beans
• 1 red pepper, halved and thinly sliced
• 50g basil leaves

Blend the chillies and garlic together using a stick blender to make a paste, or finely chop them and give them a mash in a pestle and mortar. Put a large wok or non-stick frying pan over a medium-high heat and add the olive oil. When the oil is hot, throw in the steak and fry quickly until it is just sealed all over. Scrape in all of the chilli and garlic paste, and fry for another minute until fragrant, then add the oyster sauce, soy sauce, beef stock cube and sugar. Add 250ml water, give it all a quick stir, and then add the green beans, red pepper and basil leaves. Fry, stirring all the time, for another 2–3 minutes until the vegetables are just starting to soften, and serve.

STIR-FRY BEEF WITH GINGER

BÁNH MÌ NÊN

This is a real showcase for fresh ginger – the recipe uses a lot, half of it added at the start so its raw heat is cooked off, leaving the more mellow notes; then half added right at the end for full gingery fire. It is worth using a decent cut of beef for this – it gets cooked very quickly so needs to be tender.

Serves 4

- 800g sirloin steak, thinly sliced
- 1 tablespoon soy sauce
- 1 teaspoon sea salt
- ½ tablespoon sugar
- ½ teaspoon freshly ground black pepper
- 2 tablespoons olive oil
- ½ shallot, finely chopped
- 3 garlic cloves, finely chopped
- 25g ginger, cut into very fine matchsticks
- 1 onion, halved and very thinly sliced

Put the beef in a bowl with the soy sauce, sea salt, sugar, black pepper and one tablespoon of olive oil. Mix well and put in the fridge to marinate for 30 minutes.

Put a wok or large frying pan over a high heat and add a tablespoon of olive oil. When it's good and hot, put in the shallot, garlic and half of the ginger. Keep the heat high and stir-fry for a minute, then add the marinated beef and stir-fry for another 4 minutes until it is just cooked. Finally, briskly stir in the remaining ginger and the onion. Cook until the onion is barely softened – you want it just heated through – and serve hot with steamed jasmine rice and mixed salad.

AN ARGENTINE ASADO

BUENOS AIRES CAFÉ

Unlike much of the rest of South America, the population of Argentina is mostly European in origin, in particular Italian (with around 55 per cent able to trace their roots back to somewhere on the Italian peninsula), and this is manifest in the country's cuisine, with pizza and pasta being staples of the Argentine diet.

The main ingredient, however, is meat – in particular beef from the herds that graze the rich, green grass of the Argentine Pampas, producing flesh that is uniquely flavoursome, succulent and low in cholesterol.

The traditional way of cooking meat in Argentina is to barbecue it, usually on a typical barbecue or *asado* – which is both the word for the thing you cook on and also the event itself.

A proper *asado* uses fire made with natural wood and charcoal. To prepare a charcoal barbecue put some handfuls of paper at the bottom of the grill, with kindling on top and then a little charcoal on top of that – not too much so as not to suffocate the fire. Light the paper and let it take its natural course, adding more charcoal as it gets more lively. It is important to use a good-quality charcoal – hard lumpwood charcoal is the best because it lasts longer and makes it easier to control the temperature. You may need up to about 5kg of charcoal depending on the amount of meat you intend to cook. In Argentina, they reckon on 500g of meat per person, not counting any empanadas or picadas (snacks or tapas) you might have eaten beforehand.

Be patient. Do not put the meat onto the grill until the charcoal is white-hot, and on no account put the meat anywhere near a flame. However, you must be careful that the temperature is right – it mustn't be *too* hot. The best way to test this is to hold your hand over the top of the grill; you should be able to keep it there for 2 seconds.

Argentine beef is spectacularly tender, but must still be cooked slowly for maximum flavour and tenderness. Rub rock salt into it before putting it on the grill or when you come to turn it. It's crucial to grill the meat slowly, not only to retain tenderness and flavour but also because the meat stays juicy longer, even after it has got cold – which makes it nice to nibble later on in the evening with a good glass of Malbec.

Parrillada

A typical Argentine *parrillada* or mixed grill contains a mixture of the following ingredients – you don't have to have all of this, but do try to have a mixture if you can, including a couple of cuts of beef, sausage, ribs, some chicken and, for a real touch of authenticity, some *chinchulines* or sweetbreads. Start with the sausages (chorizos, morcillas), then the *chinchulines*, leaving the best and juiciest meat for the end.

• *Bife ancho:* ribeye steak, some say the tastiest cut of all.

• *Bife de chorizo:* sirloin steak

• *Bife de lomo:* fillet steak

• Chicken: usually spatchcocked and marinated with lemon or chimichurri.

• *Chinchulines:* the most popular kind of *achuras* or offal – pork, beef or lambs' small intestines; what we would call chitterlings. They should be well crisped on the outside and soft in the middle.

- Chorizo: Buenos Aires Café make their own chorizo sausages in the restaurant, using good-quality pork and various other ingredients including Malbec wine, chilli and paprika. They are absolutely delicious and the recipe is absolutely secret, so you'll just have to drop by to try them.

- Morcilla: blood sausage or black pudding, usually pre-cooked so it doesn't need to be on the barbecue for so long.

- Pork ribs: unlike beef ribs, these are usually marinated and then cooked slowly for maximum tenderness and flavour.

- *Tira de asado:* a unique Argentine cut, where ribs are cross-cut through the bone to make long strips.

- *Vacio:* flank steak.

You'll be starting to feel hungry now you can smell the meat cooking, so this is when the Argentines would tuck into some empanadas – see page 90 for the recipe.

When the meat is ready, it is served simply with a mixed salad and some chimichurri (page 104), the herby, garlicky, slightly spicy sauce without which no Argentine barbecue would be complete.

Afters…

After all that food, desserts tend to be something easy to prepare like a crêpe, usually served with Argentinians' favourite sweet ingredient, dulce de leche – caramelised vanilla milk, sort of like runny toffee. Dulce de leche is a very important ingredient in every kitchen and restaurant in Argentina, serving as a filling for everything from morning pastries to cakes, desserts, biscuits and more or less anything else you could think of.

Mate

Like the British, Argies love a cup of tea in the afternoon, only in their case a cuppa means *mate* – a strong, bitter beverage drunk with a metal straw called a *bombilla* from a gourd-like bowl that in Argentina is also called a *mate*. The flavour is reminiscent of some varieties of green tea but it is in fact made from the leaves of the yerba plant, which is a member of the holly family. You can also buy flavoured *mate*, in which the yerba leaves are blended with herbs or other ingredients such as peppermint or lemon rind. *Mate* is super-popular in Argentina, where around 5kg of the dried leaves are consumed per person every year – and is even more loved in neighbouring Uruguay, where consumption is about twice that!

The drink is prepared by filling your *mate* or gourd about three-quarters full with dry yerba leaves and twigs, and topping it up with hot (but not boiling – usually around 70–80ºC) water. Sugar is optional. Drinking *mate* is, above all else, a social activity, something you do with friends, refilling and passing on the gourd to the next person after taking a few mouthfuls.

FISH & SEAFOOD

STAMP AND GO

(Salt fish fritters)

❧

ARAWAK GRILL

Here is Robert's take on another Jamaican classic. Who knows why they're called Stamp and Go: 'Stamp 'em out in the kitchen, take 'em and go' is one explanation (they're quick and easy to make, and are perfect travelling food); another is that customers would stamp on the floor to get the attention of the vendor before taking off with their snack. Whatever, they are perfect finger food – light, salty, and just perfect with a cold Red Stripe and some hot sauce.

Serves 4–6

- 250g salt fish
- 1 onion, finely chopped
- 1 Scotch bonnet pepper, finely chopped
- 1 garlic clove, finely chopped
- 750g plain flour
- ½ teaspoon freshly ground black pepper
- salt
- sunflower oil, for frying

Soak the salt fish overnight, or boil it for 10 minutes, drain and rinse well with cold water. Drain the fish well, then flake it with your fingers into a bowl. Add the onion, Scotch bonnet (leaving the seeds in if you like it hot) and garlic and give it a mix, then sift in the flour, a pinch of salt and the black pepper. Slowly stir in 500ml water with your fingers, stopping when you have a thick batter with a nice dropping consistency. Make sure you've mixed in any hidden pockets of flour and have broken up any big clumps of fish.

Fill a frying pan about 0.5cm deep with sunflower oil and put over a medium heat until a tiny piece of the batter sizzles as soon as it is dropped in. When it's hot enough, drop in heaped tablespoons of the batter and fry for 5–10 minutes, then turn them over and fry until they are golden brown on each side and cooked in the middle. Remove with a slotted spoon and drain on kitchen roll. Do this in batches until all the fritters are cooked. Serve piping hot with a hot sauce for dipping.

SMOKED SALMON AND GULA TAPAS

HOLA PAELLA

Gula are a strange-looking Spanish *surimi* or processed fish made from Alaskan pollock which look just like baby eels with a silvery grey stripe along the top. The most common brand is *La Gula del Norte* – they are very hard to find in the UK, but they really are worth hunting down as they have a great flavour.

Serves 4

- 100g gula
- 1 garlic clove, very finely chopped
- 1 small red chilli, thinly sliced
- 8 slices fresh baguette, toasted
- drizzle of olive oil
- 100g smoked salmon, sliced
- handful of salad leaves
- ½ lemon
- salt
- freshly ground black pepper

Drain the gula of any oil and place in a bowl with the garlic and chilli. Add a little salt and a grind of black pepper, then mix it all up well with your hands. Drizzle the toasted slices of baguette with a little olive oil. Layer the smoked salmon on top, and heap a small handful of the gula mix on top of that. Garnish with some fresh salad leaves on the side, and squeeze the half lemon over the whole plate before serving.

WOK PRAWNS WITH SALT, CHILLI AND LEMONGRASS

❧

BÁNH MÌ NÊN

Crispy fried prawns; chewy, sweet shallots; hot chilli – this is great either as a starter or just to nibble at with some beers. It's quick to cook but worth getting everything prepared before you start cooking so do all your slicing and chopping first. Potato starch is easy to find in any Chinese or Asian supermarket and makes a really crunchy and light batter.

Serves 4

- 500g king prawns, shelled
- 2 egg whites
- 100g potato starch
- 2 tablespoons olive oil
- 10g shallot, finely chopped
- 3 garlic cloves, finely chopped
- 1 onion, thinly sliced
- 2 red chillies, thinly sliced
- 1 stalk of lemongrass, thinly sliced
- bunch of spring onions, sliced
- ½ teaspoon five-spice powder
- salt
- freshly ground black pepper
- sunflower oil, for deep frying

Season the prawns with a little salt and pepper and put in the fridge. Lightly beat the egg whites and set aside, then slice and chop all your vegetables so you're ready to go.

When you're ready to eat, heat about 5cm of sunflower oil in a deep pan or wok until a cube of bread starts to sizzle and turn gold as soon as you throw it in. Turn the prawns in the egg whites, then take out and coat quickly with the potato starch. Deep fry in small batches, draining on kitchen paper when each batch is done.

Put the olive oil in a large wok (or frying pan) over a really high heat. Add the shallots and garlic and stir-fry for a minute. Add the onion, chillies and lemongrass, stir, then throw in the fried prawns and cook for about 15 seconds, stirring and shaking the pan so the flavourings and prawns get thoroughly mixed. Take off the heat, stir in the spring onions and five-spice powder and dig in.

VIETNAMESE SUMMER ROLLS WITH PRAWNS

BÁNH MÌ NÊN

Tran rolls these up in moments, each one as pretty as summer itself with glimpses of green and red and pink through the rice papers. They are very light and easy to make. You'll find the rice papers at any Chinese supermarket or Asian grocer – Red Rose and Three Ladies are both reliable brands.

Serves 4

for the peanut sauce:
- 1 tablespoon vegetable oil
- 1 shallot, finely chopped
- 4 garlic cloves, crushed
- 125g peanut butter
- 2 tablespoons hoisin sauce
- 2 teaspoons sugar
- 1 teaspoon salt

for the summer rolls:
- 1 bag rice papers
- small handful of mint
- ½ iceberg lettuce, shredded (or a bag of mixed salad)

- 100g cucumber, cut into fine matchsticks
- 100g carrot, cut into fine matchsticks
- 20g beansprouts
- small handful of coriander
- ½ red onion, finely sliced
- 150g cooked king prawns

to serve:
- sweet chilli sauce
- 2 tablespoons salted peanuts, crushed

Make the peanut sauce first. Heat the oil in a small pan and fry the shallot for a couple of minutes. Add the garlic and keep frying until it's a light gold colour, then stir in 250ml water, the peanut butter and hoisin sauce. Bring to the boil and simmer, stirring, for about 5 minutes. Add the sugar and salt, then blend the sauce to get a perfectly smooth, glossy texture. Leave to cool.

Put some cold water in a shallow bowl big enough to hold the rice papers. Dip a paper in for 3 seconds, holding it under with your fingers so both sides get wet, then shake it dry for another 3 seconds and put on a flat plate or chopping board. Build up the filling in a strip in the middle of the paper: first two or three mint leaves, then some shredded iceberg lettuce or salad, then cucumber and carrot, then beansprouts, coriander and red onion. Fold one side of the rice paper over the filling and put a row of three or four king prawns on top. Holding the filling in place, fold the sides of the paper in, then roll the whole thing up. Work quickly and don't put too much inside as it will make it hard to roll.

Serve two summer rolls per person, either with the peanut sauce or with some sweet chilli sauce and crushed salted peanuts on top.

SEA BASS AND PRAWN MOILEE

MOGUL

This is a great dish from Mogul – slightly sweet thanks to the coconut milk, but keenly spiced and aromatic with green chilli, cardamom, cloves and curry leaves. It's best served simply with some steamed rice.

Serves 2

- 200g raw prawns (cleaned and deveined)
- 300g sea bass fillets (cut into generous strips)
- ¾ teaspoon turmeric powder
- ½ teaspoon grated fresh ginger
- 1 teaspoon chilli powder
- 2 teaspoons coconut oil
- 3 cloves
- 4 green cardamom pods
- 2.5cm cinnamon stick
- 2 garlic cloves, minced
- 1 onion, thinly sliced
- 10–12 curry leaves
- 250ml coconut milk
- 1 tomato, thinly sliced
- 1 teaspoon freshly squeezed lemon juice
- 3 green chillies (if you like your food spicy, chop the chillies before adding, if not, keep whole)
- salt

Toss the prawns and sea bass in a bowl with ½ teaspoon of the turmeric, ¼ teaspoon of the grated ginger and the chilli powder. Leave for around 15 minutes for the flavours to absorb and mingle.

Heat the coconut oil in a wide, heavy pan over a low heat. When it's hot, throw in the cloves, cardamom and cinnamon and toast for 2 minutes when they should smell fragrant. Turn the heat up a bit and add the remaining grated ginger, the garlic, onion and curry leaves. Cook, stirring for another 3 minutes until the onion has started to soften, then add the remaining ¼ teaspoon of turmeric, half of the coconut milk and about ¼ teaspoon salt. Stir well to mix, then put the sliced tomato in and bring the pan to a gentle boil. Add the prawns and fish and cook until just opaque – about 5 or 6 minutes. Add the rest of the coconut milk and bring to a gentle boil, then stir in the lemon juice and green chillies. Serve immediately.

SEA BASS WITH GINGER DIPPING SAUCE AND GREEN MANGO SALAD

❧

BÁNH MÌ NÊN

This is very simple and very quick but it makes for an amazing combination of flavours: hot, crispy sea bass fillets, cool, sour green mango salad zinging with fresh herbs, and a perfectly balanced sweet, salty sauce hot with ginger and chilli.

Serves 4

- 4 sea bass fillets
- 1 green mango (about 60g)
- ½ red onion, thinly sliced
- small handful of coriander, roughly chopped
- 5 mint leaves, roughly chopped
- 2 tablespoons fish sauce
- 1 tablespoon freshly squeezed lime juice
- 2 tablespoons sugar
- 1 tablespoon finely grated fresh ginger
- ½ garlic clove, finely chopped
- 1 birds-eye chilli, finely chopped
- 2 tablespoons olive oil
- salt
- freshly ground black pepper

Lightly season the sea bass with salt and black pepper and leave aside for 15 minutes while you make the mango salad. Peel the green mango and cut in half to remove the stone. Cut the flesh into matchsticks about 3cm long and 3mm wide. Mix with the red onion, coriander and mint and put it into the fridge.

Next, make the dipping sauce: stir the fish sauce, lime juice and sugar into 250ml hot water in a bowl. Taste – if it is too salty or sour for you, then add another 50ml water. Leave to cool to room temperature, then add the ginger, garlic and chilli.

Heat the oil in a non-stick, wide frying pan over a high heat. When it's good and hot, put in the sea bass fillets skin side down (you may need to do this in batches). Cook for 3–4 minutes until the skin is crispy, then carefully turn them over and cook for another minute or so until the flesh is opaque.

Put one fillet on each plate and pour over 3 tablespoons of the dipping sauce. Top with a large spoonful of the mango salad, and serve immediately with some steamed jasmine rice and the rest of the dipping sauce in a bowl for everyone to help themselves to.

JAY'S SPICY SEA BASS

(Sengseon Tang)

❧

TERIYAKI-YA

This is a clear and bright fish dish from Jay at Teriyaki-ya. He wanted to give us a recipe for really authentic Korean home cooking, and this is one that he adapted from his grandmother's sea bass *jjigae*. *Jjigae* is a stew-like dish, made with meat, seafood or vegetables in a broth and typically served boiling hot in a communal pot. His grandmother's recipe involved stewing whole fish slowly with root vegetables like potato, carrot and mooli: Jay's version takes about 10 minutes from start to finish and cooks sea bass fillets in a light, fresh stock. Instead of root vegetables, he uses those tiny, long-stemmed, enoki mushrooms sold in clumps in Chinese supermarkets – rather magical looking, yet quite easy to find. You don't have to use sea bass – fillets of sea bream, grey mullet or any flat fish will also be delicious.

Serves 2

- 2 sea bass fillets
- 50g enoki or any other cup mushroom
- 2 tablespoons soy sauce
- 1 tablespoon mirin (or 1 tablespoon granulated sugar)
- ½ onion, finely sliced
- 1 garlic clove, finely chopped
- 1 birds-eye chilli, deseeded and finely chopped
- 1 spring onion, finely sliced
- 1 teaspoon sesame seeds
- sea salt

Put the sea bass fillets skin side down on a board and season with sea salt. If you're using enoki mushrooms, just leave them whole but trim at the base. Thinly slice if you're using any other kind.

Pour 140ml water into a pan wide enough to take both fillets and add the soy sauce and mirin (or sugar). Bring to a simmer over a low heat, then put in the fish and scatter the mushrooms, onion, garlic and chilli around the edges. Cover the pan and simmer gently for about 7 minutes, until the fish is just cooked through.

To serve, put a fish fillet on each plate, then top with some of the mushrooms and onion. Pour over some of the broth from the pan and garnish with some spring onion slices and sesame seeds. Eat with a big bowl of rice.

"WORKING ON THE MARKET IS CRAZY FUN. SETTING UP ON THE COLD, FRESH MORNINGS, GRABBING A CUPPA FOR EACH OTHER AND CHATTING WHILE STARTING YOUR DAY... SOMEONE RUNNING AROUND MID-SERVICE BEGGING FOR CHANGE...WE ALL HELP EACH OTHER OUT AS BEST WE CAN..."

Fay, *Victus & Bibo*

VEGGIE

CHEESE TOASTY

୭ଌ

TURNIPS

Any Saturday morning the windows at Turnips are piled high with these, waiting to be toasted for their queue of toasty fans. It's a pretty simple formula: really good bread + really good cheese + plenty of alliums = super tasty.

Serves 1

• 50g Montgomery Cheddar cheese, grated
• a few slices of leek, finely chopped
• 2 spring onions, finely chopped
• 2 slices sourdough bread
• 1 teaspoon olive oil

Put the cheese in a bowl and mix in the leek and spring onions. Pile onto a slice of the bread, then clap the other slice on top. Drizzle the outsides of the sandwich with a little olive oil then put in a toasty maker or under the grill until the cheese is oozing out of the sides and the bread is extra golden and crispy.

MUSHROOMS ON TOAST

❧

TURNIPS

Mushrooms on toast, when made Turnips-style, is the simplest and tastiest way of showing off a bag of mixed wild mushrooms to their very best. Herb-wise you can use whatever you fancy, either keep it simple with flat-leaf parsley, or try something different – dill and thyme both love mushrooms.

Serves 1

• 1 tablespoon olive oil
• a knob of butter
• 1 garlic clove, finely chopped
• 100g wild mushrooms (mixture of any), sliced if they're big
• 1 slice good sourdough bread
• a few tablespoons of flat-leaf parsley, roughly chopped
• salt
• freshly ground black pepper

Melt the olive oil and butter in frying pan over a medium heat. Fry the garlic for a moment or two until it softens, then throw in the mushrooms, season with salt and lots of freshly ground black pepper and sauté until soft and golden. Meanwhile, lightly toast your slice of sourdough bread. When the mushrooms are cooked, add the parsley, give it a quick stir and pile onto the toast. Devour.

"WE'RE FAMOUS FOR OUR FRESH JUICES AND CHEESE TOASTIES – WE SELL HUNDREDS ON A GOOD DAY. THE TRICK IS USING GREAT SOURDOUGH AND REALLY GOOD FARMHOUSE CHEDDAR, WHICH WE GET FROM NEAL'S YARD DAIRY." Jamie, *Turnips*

ARTICHOKE AND IDIAZABAL SALAD

❧

HOLA PAELLA

Hard to say which is the true star ingredient in this lovely salad from Carrie at Hola Paella. The roasted piquillo peppers, sweet and satin soft? Or the shavings of waxy, smoky Idiazabal cheese? Either way, it's a fantastic lunch dish, easy to throw together, easy to eat. You can find both Idiazabal and roasted piquillo peppers in most Spanish delis.

Serves 2 as a main course, 4 as a starter

- 8 roasted artichoke hearts in olive oil
- 200g roasted piquillo peppers from a jar
- handful of pitted black olives
- ¼ teaspoon dried Spanish oregano
- 2 big handfuls of salad leaves
  (Carrie suggests a mix of rocket, baby spinach and some oak-leaf lettuce)
- juice of ½ lemon
- 100g Idiazabal smoked cheese
- salt
- freshly ground black pepper

Cut each artichoke heart lengthwise into four slices. Cut the piquillo peppers in half and then thinly slice them lengthwise. Cut the olives in half. Mix the artichokes, piquillo peppers and olives in a large bowl and sprinkle half the dried oregano on top, and a bit of salt and black pepper. Add the salad leaves and give it a quick mix, then drizzle with the lemon juice to taste. The artichokes bring enough oil to the salad, so you won't need to add more. Shave off some thin slivers of the Idiazabal cheese and scatter them generously on top of the salad – you could use a potato peeler for this. Scatter over the remaining oregano and a bit more black pepper and you're ready to go.

CALÇOTS CON SALSA ROMESCO

∽✦∽

HOLA PAELLA

The calçot is a big deal in Catalonia, so much so that there are huge outdoor feasts or calçotadas to celebrate its harvest. Calçots are essentially large sweet spring onions or green onions, only available from December to early May and traditionally cooked over burning vines and served with bowls of romesco sauce to dip them into.

No need to miss out on their pleasures just because you're not in Catalonia: this is still really good with ordinary spring onions, just make sure they are as large as possible. Don't worry about any leftover romesco sauce, it is great as an accompaniment for meats, or just as a dip with toasted bread.

Serves 4

- 60ml olive oil
- 60g slice of crusty bread, torn into pieces
- 125g blanched almonds, chopped or slivered
- 5–6 garlic cloves, chopped
- 1 × 400g tin chopped tomatoes

- 1 large red pepper, roasted and peeled (or a 250g jar of roasted red peppers, drained)
- 1 tablespoon smoked paprika
- 2–3 tablespoons sherry vinegar
- 1 teaspoon salt
- 24 large spring onions (or calçots, if you can find them)

First make the romesco sauce.

Preheat the oven to 180ºC. Heat the olive oil in a frying pan over a medium-high heat. When the oil is hot, fry the bread and almonds until they just begin to brown – keep stirring so they don't burn. Add the garlic and fry for another couple of minutes, stirring once or twice.

Put the contents of the frying pan into a food processor with the tomatoes, roasted red pepper, smoked paprika, vinegar and salt. Blitz until you have a thick, smooth sauce, then spread it in an even layer on a rimmed baking tray. Bake in the oven for 20 minutes or until the edges begin to caramelise, then scrape the whole lot into a serving bowl and give it a stir.

Next, roast your calçots – ideally they should be cooked on a flaming barbecue but if that's not possible you can put them under a hot grill or fry them with a little oil in a griddle pan. In both cases, cook until the outer skins are black and smoky, then wrap them in newspaper for 5 minutes to cool down and steam to perfect tenderness.

To eat, pull off the blackened skin and dip in the romesco sauce. This is very messy but very tasty finger food.

"GREENWICH IN GENERAL FEELS LIKE A VILLAGE, WHICH IS AMAZING CONSIDERING HOW MANY TOURISTS IT ATTRACTS. IT SOMEHOW FEELS SLIGHTLY REMOVED FROM THE BIG SMOKE THAT IS LONDON. THE MARKET ITSELF IS LIKE A BIG FAMILY, WITH ALL ITS UPS AND DOWNS BUT WITH AN UNDERLYING SENSE OF LOYALTY AND CARE THAT IS VITAL TO ITS APPEAL."

Carrie, *Hola Paella*

COGOLLOS CON QUESO DE CABRALES

❧

HOLA PAELLA

Or, chicory boats filled with a double cream and Cabrales mash… This is another of Carrie's delicious tapas, starring one of Spain's most celebrated cheeses: Cabrales. It's a blue cheese from Asturias, aged in the limestone caves of the Picos de Europa mountains and traditionally wrapped in maple leaves. You can usually get it at Hola Paella – it is strong and acidic and salty and works brilliantly with the bitter crunch of chicory.

Serves 4

• 1 head chicory
• 150g Cabrales cheese
• 8 tablespoons extra-thick double cream
• 10 slices fresh baguette, cut on the diagonal
• drizzle of olive oil
• 10–15 cherry tomatoes, halved
• handful of parsley, finely chopped
• salt
• freshly ground black pepper

Separate the chicory leaves, then gently wash and dry them. Break the Cabrales into small pieces and mash it up with the cream in a large mixing bowl (this will be much easier if the cheese is at room temperature). Taste the mixture and season to taste with salt and pepper – you also might want to add some more cream as the cheese is pretty strong. Pile about three teaspoons of the cheese cream mash into each chicory leaf.

Lightly grill the bread on both sides, then put it on a plate and drizzle with a little olive oil. Lay a filled chicory leaf on each slice, and garnish with two or three tomato halves and a little chopped parsley. Give everything a good grind of black pepper and serve.

CHICKPEA SALAD WITH TOMATO SAUCE AND WAKAME SEAWEED

❧

RETURN TO SHASHAMANE

Emilia's chickpea salad has a multi-layered depth of flavour: a sweet, vegetable-rich sauce, with the salt-savoury kick of wakame seaweed. Serve cold for a great vegetable-protein hit!

Serves 4–6

- 250g dried chickpeas (or 2 × 400g tins)
- 1 bay leaf
- 3 peppercorns
- 2 red peppers
- 2 large carrots, chopped into large chunks
- 1 tablespoon sunflower oil

- 1 onion, finely chopped
- ½ teaspoon paprika (sweet or smoked)
- 1 teaspoons coriander seeds
- 300g tinned chopped tomatoes
- 1 strand wakame seaweed
- 1 teaspoon mustard seeds
- salt

If using dried chickpeas, soak them in plenty of cold water overnight or for at least 8 hours. Drain, and put into a large pan with the bay leaf, peppercorns and a pinch of salt. Cover with water, bring to the boil and simmer until absolutely soft – this can take 1–2 hours depending on the age of your beans.

While the beans are cooking, make the sauce. Preheat the oven to 200ºC, and put the red peppers on a baking tray. Roast them for 30 minutes, turning every so often, until they are soft and slightly charred. Put the peppers in a bowl, sprinkle with salt and leave them until they are cool enough to be handled. Then peel the skin off, remove the stalk and seeds and blitz them in a food processor. Boil the carrots in plenty of water until very tender, then drain and finely chop.

Put the sunflower oil in a large pan over a medium heat. Add the onion and fry until soft but not coloured, then stir in the paprika and the coriander seeds – Emilia keeps them whole for a bit of texture, but if you want a stronger flavour you could grind them before adding. Add the peppers and carrots, then stir in the tomatoes and leave it all to simmer on a low heat for about 30 minutes. Add salt according to taste and leave to cool.

Drain the chickpeas and stir them into the tomato pepper sauce. Put the wakame seaweed and a pinch of salt into a small bowl and cover with water. Leave to soak for 10 minutes or so, then take out the seaweed and chop it roughly before mixing into the chickpeas. Just before serving, stir in the mustard seeds.

VIETNAMESE MANGO SALAD

❧

BÁNH MÌ NÊN

Green mangos – those hard, sticky, kidney-shaped ones that fit in the palm of your hand – are a wonderful thing. You'll find them in most Asian grocers' shops and they're very straightforward to deal with. The skin peels off easily with a potato peeler, and the dense flesh underneath is a beautiful pale pistachio colour with a strong, fruity but sour smell, like fragrant turpentine. Slice them in half and the soft stone should be easy to slip out with the point of a knife. They're eaten with enthusiasm all over South East Asia – sometimes just dipped in chilli, salt and sugar, sometimes sprinkled with soy sauce, and often grated into pickles and salads. This colourful salad from Tran at Bánh Mì Nên is a great way to use them: salty, sour, fruity and spicy. You could stir in 200g cooked prawns at the end, but it's at its best served cold with a bag of prawn crackers and some beer.

Serves 4

• 2 young green mangos (weighing about 60g each)
• 1 carrot
• 1 red onion
• small handful of coriander, roughly chopped
• 2 sprigs mint, roughly chopped
• 50g roasted salted peanuts, roughly chopped
• 1 tablespoon fish sauce
• 1½ tablespoons sugar
• 1 tablespoon freshly squeezed lime juice
• 1–3 green chillies (according to taste), finely chopped
• 1 bag prawn crackers

Wash and peel the green mangos and the carrot, then cut them into matchsticks about 3cm long and 3mm wide. Slice the onion into paper-thin half-moons. Mix with the coriander, mint and peanuts in a large bowl.

To make the dressing, mix the fish sauce, sugar, lime juice and chillies in a bowl, stirring until the sugar has dissolved. Then dress the salad to taste, starting with a tablespoon and adding more if your mangos are really sour.

Serve in a bowl with the prawn crackers on the side.

ONION BHAJIS

❧

MOGUL

Slightly caramelised fried onions, barely held together by a light and fragrant herby batter – these are not at all like the indifferent, soggy things you may be used to getting with your takeaway, and are very satisfying to make.

Makes about 25

- 500g onions, thinly sliced
- 100g gram (chickpea) flour
- 1 tablespoon ginger and garlic paste
- 1 tablespoon chopped coriander
- 2 spring onions, roughly chopped
- 2–3 green chillies, finely chopped (optional)
- 1 teaspoon ground fennel seeds
- 1 teaspoon cumin powder
- 1½ tablespoons freshly squeezed lemon juice
- salt
- vegetable oil, for frying

Mix the onions, gram flour, ginger and garlic paste, coriander, spring onions, chillies, fennel, cumin and lemon juice until you have a smooth but thick paste. Add 50–100ml water if necessary: you don't want it to be too soggy, just wet enough that the bhaji paste coats the onions thickly when a small clump is held in your fingertips. Add salt to taste and leave to stand for 20 minutes.

Pour 5cm of vegetable oil into a deep pan or wok and heat to 190–200°C (hot, but not smoking) over a medium heat. Prepare a tray covered with absorbent paper and place it next to the hot pan. Gently lower clumps of the onion mixture into the hot oil with a slotted spoon – you can probably fit in three or four at a time, but don't fry too many at once or you'll lower the heat of the oil. After 2 minutes, turn the bhajis over to cook the other side then remove with a slotted spoon when they are golden all over. Put them on the absorbent paper to drain any excess oil and eat while hot, with chutney.

COURGETTE SOUP

HOLA PAELLA

This is a lovely, elegant soup for summer – the palest pistachio colour, gently but firmly flavoured. Delicious, and a good way of dealing with a courgette glut.

Serves 4

- 30g butter
- 1 tablespoon sunflower oil
- 3 onions, chopped
- 1kg courgettes, diced
- 1 litre hot chicken stock
- 200ml crème fraîche
- fresh nutmeg, grated
- drizzle of walnut oil
- salt
- freshly ground black pepper

Heat the butter and oil in a big pan and sweat the onions gently until they are soft and translucent. Add the courgettes, cover the pan and let them soften. Sprinkle over a bit of salt and, if you think it needs it, a knob more butter. Pour the chicken stock into the pan, bring to a simmer and cook, covered, for 15–20 minutes.

Take the soup off the heat and use a stick blender to whizz it to a creamy consistency. Stir in the crème fraîche, and season with salt, plenty of freshly ground black pepper and lots of nutmeg. Add a splash of walnut oil to finish.

PISTO

(Mixed Fried Vegetables)

❧

TORTILLA'S HOME

'Mixed fried vegetables' really undersells this wonderful Spanish dish that Jose serves with his tortillas at Tortilla's Home. It's a meld of Mediterranean vegetables, cooked slowly to a sweet softness in olive oil, robust and flavourful and wonderful eaten with good bread, dried meats and cheese, or with an egg poached on top.

Serves 4

• 5 tablespoons extra virgin olive oil
• 1 onion, thinly sliced
• 1 red pepper, thinly sliced
• 1 green pepper, thinly sliced
• 1 courgette, thinly sliced
• 1 aubergine, halved and sliced
• 1 large tomato, roughly chopped
• 2 teaspoons brown sugar (optional)
• salt

Pour the olive oil into a large pan, and put on a medium heat. Throw in the onions and peppers with about ½ teaspoon of salt and fry until they start to soften – about 10 minutes. Add the courgette, stir and fry, then a couple of minutes later throw in the aubergine. Turn the heat down a bit and let it all cook together until the vegetables are so soft you can break them up with a wooden spoon. Add the tomato and, if you're using it, the brown sugar, then cover the pan and let it cook for another 10 minutes until the tomato has cooked right down. Add more salt to taste and serve either hot or at room temperature.

TORTILLA DE PATATAS

∾

TORTILLA'S HOME

At his stall, Jose turns out hundreds of individual juicy little tortillas topped with all manner of things from fried eggs to vegetarian *Pisto* (page 76). This recipe is for a larger tortilla, and is absolutely traditional. It might look enormous for four people, but you will alarm yourself by how much you can eat in a sitting.

Serves 4

• 400ml extra virgin olive oil, plus 2 tablespoons for frying
• 1.1kg potatoes, peeled and sliced
• 300g onions, sliced
• 5 eggs
• ½ teaspoon salt

Heat the olive oil in a very large pan over a medium heat. When it is good and hot, throw in the potatoes and onions and cook them, covered, until they are soft but before they take on much colour – this can take up to 20 minutes. Stir occasionally to make sure the potatoes are cooking evenly and nothing is sticking to the bottom of the pan. Once the potatoes and onions are ready, drain off the oil and put them in a bowl.

Break the eggs into another bowl and beat with the salt, then pour them into the potato and onion mix and gently stir so everything is well combined. Add 2 tablespoons of oil to a large non-stick frying pan. Put over a medium heat, and when the oil is hot, pour the tortilla mix into the pan and shake to help it settle. Leave to cook for 5–10 minutes – pull the sides away from the pan to see if the bottom is cooked, then flip it over by sliding the tortilla on to a large plate, inverting the pan over the uncooked top and flipping the whole thing over so the cooked side is uppermost. Cook for another 10 minutes (poke a knife into the middle to make sure the middle isn't too runny) before sliding it onto a plate and serving.

MACARONI CHEESE

~

PIG DOGS AND BRISKET

Not just any old mac and cheese... Topped with an amazing sweet, spicy, salty topping ingeniously made of crumbled bacon and breadcrumbs, and smooth and unctuous underneath – you think it's going to be too rich, too filling, too everything, and then the next thing you know you've eaten half the dish. Serve with BBQ Pork Belly (page 30) and Pickled Watermelon (page 107).

Serves 4

for the topping:
- 3 tablespoons olive oil
- 3 rashers smoked streaky bacon
- 1 garlic clove, crushed
- 100g fresh breadcrumbs
- 50g BBQ Rub (page 105)
- 100g Cheddar cheese, grated

for the macaroni cheese:
- 500g dried macaroni
- 50g butter
- 1 garlic clove, crushed
- 2 bay leaves
- 1 sprig fresh thyme, leaves only
- 50g plain flour
- 500ml whole milk
- 150g Gruyère cheese, grated
- 150g Cheddar cheese, grated

Preheat the oven to 180ºC and then get started on the topping.

Heat the oil in a large frying pan and fry the bacon until very crispy on both sides. Add the garlic and breadcrumbs, and continue to fry until the breadcrumbs are golden, then set aside and allow to cool.

Transfer the bacon and breadcrumb mixture to a food processor. Add the BBQ Rub and blitz until you have coarse crumbs, then add the cheese and blitz for a second or two more to thoroughly mix. Set aside.

Bring a large pan of salted water to the boil and cook the macaroni for 10 minutes or so or until al dente. Drain, refresh in cold water, then drain again and shake well to remove any excess water.

Melt the butter in the same pan that you used to cook the macaroni. Once it's melted, add the garlic, bay leaves and thyme and cook gently over a medium-low heat for a minute or two. Stir in the flour and continue to cook for a couple of minutes until a light, straw-coloured roux is formed. With the pan still on the heat, slowly pour in the milk, whisking gently to remove any lumps. Cook until it thickens to a smooth bubbling sauce, stirring all the time. Pass through a fine sieve to remove the bay and thyme, then stir in the Gruyère and Cheddar and the drained macaroni.

Pour the mixture into a large ovenproof dish and cover with the topping. Bake in the oven for 20 minutes until it is golden brown and bubbling.

STUFFED AUBERGINES

❦

VEGAN GARDEN

This old vegetarian staple is given new life by Vegan Garden's Kaya. A silky-soft slipper of aubergine, stuffed to the gunnels with rice and veggies, full of the flavours of the Mediterranean.

Serves 4

- 150g rice (brown, white, black – any type is fine)
- 2 large aubergines
- 4 tablespoons olive oil
- 1 tomato, roughly chopped
- 100g courgette, roughly chopped
- 60g onion, roughly chopped
- handful of olives, roughly chopped
- large handful of parsley, roughly chopped
- salt
- freshly ground black pepper

Preheat the oven to 200°C.

Bring a large pan of salted water to the boil, then throw in the rice and cook for 10–20 minutes depending on the kind of rice you are using – it should be just tender. When it's done, drain and leave to cool in the sieve.

Meanwhile, cut the aubergines in half lengthwise and scoop out the flesh, leaving a shell about 1cm thick. Roughly chop the scoopings. Heat 3 tablespoons of the olive oil in a wide frying pan over a medium heat, and fry the aubergine flesh for 10 minutes or so until it is soft and golden. Tip it into a large bowl with the rice, tomato, courgette, onion, olives and parsley and mix everything up with your hands. Season to taste with salt and plenty of freshly ground black pepper – the filling needs to be highly seasoned.

Brush the insides of the aubergine shells with the remaining tablespoon of olive oil and put them on a baking tray, then pile in the filling. Cover with foil and bake for an hour, then take off the foil and bake for another 10 minutes so the tops are golden and crispy.

BROWN LENTILS

ETHIOPIAN VEGETARIAN FOOD

You don't see Ethiopian food in many markets, and Helen's stall at Greenwich is a real find. Her food sings with simple clean flavours: tiny, crispy samosas so hot from the fryer you need to juggle them; warming, spicy chickpeas; a wonderfully soothing lentil and spinach soup, golden with turmeric. And these lovely little brown lentils, cooked simply with garlic, ginger and turmeric – guaranteed to turn around any cold winter's day.

Serves 4

• 4 tablespoons sunflower oil
• 2 onions, finely chopped
• 3 tomatoes, finely chopped
• 3 garlic, finely chopped
• thumb-sized piece of fresh ginger, grated
• 1 teaspoon turmeric
• 250g brown lentils
• salt

Heat the sunflower oil in a large saucepan over a medium heat, and throw in the onions. Fry them until they are very soft and golden, then add the tomatoes, garlic, ginger and turmeric. Give it all a good stir, add a pinch of salt, and fry for another 5 minutes until the tomatoes have cooked down a bit and the fragrances are starting to sing. Pour in 1.2 litres of water, then add the lentils. Bring to the boil, then turn the heat down and leave to simmer for 45 minutes to 1 hour – the cooking time will vary according to the age of your lentils so if they're not tender, give them a little bit longer. Add salt to taste and serve with rice and maybe some spinach on the side.

DOUGH & PASTRY

INSPIRATIONAL PASTRY DOUGH

❧

L'ARTISAN

Dustin of L'Artisan is evangelical about cooking. His big pies and tarts look like something from a children's book: great golden glistening things, packed with all kinds of deliciousness, the pastry crumbly but strong enough to keep the fillings reined in.

His biggest bugbear is people's fear of getting stuck in and trying to cook stuff for themselves, and so he's passed on his dough recipe – it forms the basis of so many dishes that it's one of the building blocks of being able to cook. 'Pastry has the reputation of being difficult to make – but this recipe is what you need to shrug off your fears. It doesn't have a fancy name and you don't need any fancy techniques to pull it off. You'd be surprised how easy it is.' It's a great recipe precisely because it breaks so many of the perceived 'rules' of pastry making (keep everything cold, don't overwork the dough) and produces a wonderful robust crust.

A few of Dustin's tips on making dough: find a table that isn't too high to work on – a high table doesn't allow you to use your body weight when you work the dough. Make sure you have a large surface to work on as you will be making a mess! The more you do it, the less mess you make...

Makes about 500g

- 280g plain flour
- 2 small eggs
- 150g soft unsalted butter, cut into 1cm pieces
- ½ teaspoon salt

Get out the biggest mixing bowl you have and sift in the flour. Crack the eggs into the bowl, then drop in the pieces of butter and the salt. Add 1 tablespoon of water, and start to mix with your hands: hold the bowl with your left hand, and scoop and mix the ingredients together with your right. When everything is roughly mixed in, it will look like very coarse crumbs with the odd lump of butter showing: squeeze these together and turn the ball of pastry dough out onto a well-floured surface. Here comes the really untraditional part: knead the dough with the heel of your hand until it is all a homogenous yellow buttery colour. Wrap it in clingfilm and put it in the fridge for 30 minutes to rest before using.

This pastry is the perfect base for a tart or a quiche, and is great for making a classic Cornish pasty and large pies – basically, any recipe that asks for pastry.

EMPANADAS DE JAMON Y QUESO

*(Ham and
Cheese Pasties)*

෴

BUENOS AIRES CAFÉ

This is a classic Argentine snack – basically a pastry case stuffed with all manner of delicious savoury ingredients – but empanadas actually originate from Galicia, north-west Spain (just like many Argentinians). Fillings depend on which part of the country you're in: some provinces use chicken, coastal areas prefer fish, while ham and cheese, vegetables and, of course, meat (usually ground beef) are popular everywhere. They're the perfect thing to eat while you're waiting for your asado to cook (page 45).

Makes 25–30

for the dough:
- 500g plain flour, plus extra for dusting
- 1 teaspoon salt
- 100g butter, diced
- 3 eggs
- 2–4 tablespoons milk

for the filling:
- 300g cheese (Cheddar or anything you prefer), cut into small cubes
- 300g ham, cut into small cubes
- 2 tablespoons grated Parmesan cheese
- 2 eggs
- salt
- freshly ground black pepper

Pile the flour and salt onto a marble slab or kitchen worktop and make a hollow in the middle. Put the butter and eggs into the hollow, then rub them into the flour with your fingertips. Add the milk, tablespoon by tablespoon, stopping when you have a smooth dough, then cover it with a tea towel and leave to rest at room temperature for 30 minutes.

While the pastry is resting, make the filling: put the cheese, ham and eggs into a bowl and mix thoroughly with your hands. Season to taste, and if the mixture looks too thick add another egg – it should be quite loose.

Flour a worktop and roll the dough out as thinly as you can – 1–2mm is perfect. Stamp out circles of about 12cm diameter. Take a heaped tablespoon of the filling and put it in the centre of a pastry circle, then fold over one side of the circle to make a half-moon shape. Twist and pinch the edges to seal them – the pastry is so thin you won't need to use any water or egg yolk.

When the pastries are all filled, you can either deep-fry them until they are a beautiful golden brown, or bake at 180ºC for about 20 minutes. If you're baking them, space them out on a floured baking tray and brush the tops with egg yolk first.

JAMAICAN PATTIES

∾

COOPIE-COCO

Alshon Higgins grew up in the tiny parish of Saint Mary in Jamaica, and was taught to cook by his grandmother there. On his stall at Greenwich he mostly sells beautiful, intense chocolates and truffles (he didn't learn them from his grandma, but on a chocolatier course in London), but he always has some of these golden, lightly spiced beef or chicken patties for sale as well.

Traditionally, the distinctive yellow colouring in the patty pastry comes from ruku or annatto seeds. In London, Alshon uses yellow food colouring or curry powder, and you could also use a touch of turmeric. Ideally you need to start this the day before you want to eat them so the filling can sit overnight to firm up and the flavours get a chance to develop. If you don't have time and do have an urgent need for patties (it can happen), a couple of hours should do.

Makes 6

for the filling:
- 250g beef braising steak or skinless chicken breast
- 1 beef, chicken or vegetable stock cube
- 4 spring onions, finely chopped
- sprig of thyme, leaves only
- ½–1 Scotch bonnet chilli, deseeded and finely chopped
- ½ teaspoon ground allspice

- 120g fresh breadcrumbs
- salt

for the pastry:
- ½ teaspoon salt
- 1 tablespoon curry powder or turmeric
- 500g plain flour
- 170g butter
- 50ml milk

The day before you want to eat the patties, put the meat in a saucepan and just cover with water. Bring to the boil, then turn down the heat and simmer for 15–20 minutes until the meat is cooked through. Remove the meat (saving the cooking water for later) and chop roughly. Put the meat into a food processor and pulse a few times until it is finely minced (if you're using beef, this will probably take a bit longer – 15 seconds or so).

Dissolve the stock cube in the water you cooked the meat in, and add the spring onions, thyme leaves, chilli and allspice. Stir in the minced meat and mix well, then add the breadcrumbs so you have a thickish, dropping consistency. Once the breadcrumbs are in, keep folding and stirring for 3 minutes to help the mixture cool down. Check for seasoning and add salt if to taste, then put in the fridge overnight to firm up.

The next day, make your pastry: in a large bowl mix the salt and curry powder or turmeric into the flour, then rub in the butter until you have the texture of breadcrumbs. Add some water, bit by bit, until it comes together in a dough – start with 100ml then add a bit more as needed. Form the pastry into a thick round, wrap it in clingfilm and leave in the fridge for 30 minutes to an hour.

Preheat the oven to 150°C and line a baking tray with greaseproof paper. Flour your work surface and roll the pastry out nice and thin – about 2mm. Using a 20cm plate as a guide, cut out as many rounds as you can, then gather up the scraps and roll out again.

Put 2–3 tablespoons of the filling in the centre of each round, then brush the edges of the pastry with milk. Fold over the pastry to make half-moon patties and crimp around the edges with a fork to seal. Put the patties on the baking tray, lightly brush them all with the remaining milk and bake in the oven for 30 minutes or until the pastry is a beautiful pale gold colour and the patties are smelling nice. And you're ready to eat!

PIZZA

❧

FORNO VIAGGIANTE PIZZERIA

The pizza dough recipe Giancarlo uses in his Citroën van is, quite rightly, a very closely guarded secret that he learnt from a pizza master in Naples and cannot share with anyone. Instead he has given us the recipe that he uses at home, which means you'll be able to get somewhere close to the southern Italy vibe even if you don't have a wood-fired oven handy.

Serves 4

- 3.5g dried yeast (half a sachet)
- 1 teaspoon sugar
- 500g '00' grade flour
- 1 teaspoon olive oil
- 1½ teaspoons salt

Sprinkle the yeast and sugar into 330ml lukewarm water and stir quickly with a fork. Leave it to activate for 5 minutes, by which time it should have a head of foam.

Put the flour in the bowl of a mixer, or in a large bowl. Pour in the yeast and water mixture, add the olive oil and then begin to knead. If you're using a mixer, use a dough hook and mix on medium for 5 minutes, before adding the salt and mixing for another 10 minutes. If you're doing it by hand (which is easy, don't worry), mix in the liquid with your hands, then tip out the shaggy dough onto a floured work surface and knead for 5 minutes before adding the salt. Knead for another 10 minutes at least until you have a soft but springy dough that doesn't stick to your worktop.

Put the dough in a large bowl and cover it with a damp tea towel, then leave it to rise for about 2 hours (the long rise pays dividends in terms of flavour). Once the dough has doubled in volume, punch it down, give it a quick knead on a floured worktop and divide it into four equal pieces. Preheat your oven to its highest setting.

Roll the pizzas out nice and thin and put on lightly oiled baking sheets. Then put on whatever toppings you like (see the next page for Giancarlo's suggestions: his absolute favourite is a margherita made with *fior di latte* mozzarella) and put in the oven to cook for 12–15 minutes, until the crust is golden and the toppings are bubbling away.

TOPPINGS

Note: Giancarlo uses the simplest tomato sauce – best-quality tinned tomatoes (preferably San Marzano pomodori pelati) crushed to a pulp with his hands.

Pulled pork
Pulled pork, mozzarella, Gorgonzola and fresh thyme. Strew with rocket as soon as it's out of the oven.

Tomatissimo
Tomato sauce, sun-dried tomatoes, cherry tomatoes, mozzarella and dollops of good pesto.

Classic margherita
Tomato sauce, *fior di latte* mozzarella, oregano and extra virgin olive oil. Finish with a leaf of basil once it's cooked.

Prosciutto e funghi
Tomato sauce, mozzarella, prosciutto, sliced mushrooms and black olives.

Quattro formaggi
Mozzarella, goat's cheese, Gorgonzola, Parmesan cheese.

Calabrese
Tomato sauce, mozzarella, homemade meatballs, nduja spicy sausage, sliced fresh chillies.

Zucchini
A courgette sliced diagonally, caramelised onion, Gorgonzola. Finish with a tablespoon of pesto sauce and shavings of Parmesan cheese just before you serve.

Vegetariana
Tomato sauce, mozzarella, slices of red onion, courgette, sweet potato and red or green peppers, black olives.

GUO TIE

*(Pan-fried
Pork Dumplings)*

LA-MIAN & DIM SUM

Originally from north-east China, these delicious pan-fried dumplings are now a staple across the whole country, and are also becoming increasingly popular internationally, especially in areas with a large ethnic Chinese population. Indeed, while it's la-mian (hand-pulled noodles) that Kelly and Zhongyi's stall is perhaps most famous for, these addictive pork dumplings are actually their biggest sellers.

Kelly and Zhongyi make their guo tie quite big, around 8–10cm in length, but you can make yours any size really. Don't try and make these dumplings in a hurry though: if you make your own wrappers, the whole process will take at least 2 hours. If you'd rather buy ready-made wrappers, make sure you get the circular (not the square) ones.

Serves 4 as a main, 6 as a starter (makes around 40 dumplings)

for the homemade wrappers:
- 375g plain flour
- 1 teaspoon salt

for the filling:
- 450g pork mince
- 6 spring onions, finely chopped
- 1–2 tablespoons grated fresh ginger
- 1 tablespoon light soy sauce
- 2 tablespoons sesame oil
- 1 teaspoon salt

- 1 teaspoon pepper
- 1 teaspoon vegetable or chicken stock powder
- sunflower, vegetable, rapeseed or peanut oil, for frying

for the dipping sauce:
- finely chopped garlic
- light soy sauce
- black or white Chinese vinegar
- sesame oil
- chilli oil

Put the kettle on. Place the flour in a large mixing bowl and add the salt. When the water just comes to a boil, slowly add 225ml bit by bit to the flour and mix with chopsticks to form a crumbly paste (add more or less water as necessary). Now, use your hands to bring together into a rough dough and then turn out onto a floured surface. Knead the dough for around 10 minutes, using a stretching and folding method as opposed to how you would normally knead bread: remember, you're not trying to get any air into the dough. Wrap with clingfilm and set aside to rest for about 1 hour.

While the dough is resting, make your filling. Combine the ingredients in a large bowl and mix well.

When the dough has rested for about an hour, remove the clingfilm and knead for a few minutes more. The dough should now have the super-soft consistency of your earlobe – try it and see! If it's not quite soft enough, leave to rest for 15–20 minutes longer.

Using a knife, cut the dough into four equal pieces, and then roll each of these pieces into a sausage around 4cm in diameter. Cut each sausage into 4cm-thick slices.

Now it's time to make the dumplings! Take a dough ball and flatten with your palm, and then take a small rolling pin (or use a bottle) and roll out to form a disc 8–10cm in diameter, and about 2–3mm thick. If you're feeling very skilled, try to make your wrappers slighter thinner at the edges: this will ensure that your filling will be well-wrapped but your folds not overly thick. Lightly flour each wrapper and set aside.

Once you have rolled out all your wrappers, it's time to fill them. Take a wrapper in the palm of your left hand, dab your right first finger in a little cold water, and rub this around the edge of the wrapper (although if your dough is fresh and moist, the water may not be necessary). Place a rounded teaspoon of the filling in the very centre of the wrapper. Now, using your thumb and first finger, take the wrapper at 12 o'clock and 6 o'clock, and pinch together firmly over the filling. You should now have a half-moon shape with the left and right edges still open. Use your thumb and first finger to pleat the wrapper edge closest to you at 1cm intervals, pinching it against the edge at the back to seal the dumpling. The shape of the finished dumpling should resemble a crescent moon, with the pleated seam along the top. (This wrapping technique is not as complicated as it sounds but just takes practice – there are plenty of tutorials online which can help you to refine your skills!)

As each dumpling is finished, place pleated side up on a floured tray. Repeat until all the filling or wrappers are used up – any leftover filling or wrappers can be frozen. You can also freeze any uncooked dumplings and cook from frozen.

To cook, heat a large flat-bottomed frying pan with a lid and add about 2 tablespoons of oil. Have the lid of the frying pan and a cup of cold water to hand. Once the pan is very hot, turn the heat down to medium and, one by one, carefully place the dumplings, pleated side up, in the pan. Once the pan is full, put the lid on and fry over a medium heat for around 5 minutes. Check that the dumplings have all browned on the underside, and now carefully add cold water to a depth of about 1cm. Cover the pan again, turn the heat up to high and continue to cook for another 5 minutes.

Test one of the dumplings to see if both the filling and the wrapper are cooked; if they're not, add a little more water. Once the dumplings are well-steamed, uncover and cook for couple more minutes, to evaporate any remaining water and to re-crisp the dumplings. Once cooked, move all the dumplings to a tray, and if necessary make another batch. Serve hot and let each person make their own little bowl of dipping sauce to their own personal taste.

BUTTER AND SAGE RAVIOLI FILLED WITH SPINACH AND RICOTTA

(Ravioli Fatti in Casa Conditi con Burro e Salvia)

IMBERT STREET FOOD

David, in his apron and bowler hat, is always a welcome sight at the market – a true pasta enthusiast, he cooks up gnocchi, arancini, and the most wonderful homemade pasta. Ravioli is one of his enthusiasms: partly because of its history, partly because of its adaptability. Legend tells, he says, how it was first invented in 1200AD at the Raviolo family inn in Genoa, and how it is mentioned in Giovanni Boccaccio's Decameron ('...they did nothing but make pasta and ravioli and cook them...') written in 1353. Since then ravioli has taken on endless regional variations – filled with meat or ricotta in Lazio, Marche and Tuscany, or formed into different shapes and becoming fagottini (little bundles), mezzelune (half-moons) or cappelletti (little caps). Even the sauce adds variety: the delicious butter, sage and Parmesan cheese sauce here could easily be switched for a simple tomato sauce. Making homemade pasta isn't something for a quick weeknight dinner: it's a leisurely weekend activity and utterly satisfying – give it a try.

Serves 4–6

- 400g '00' grade flour
- 5 eggs
- 200g spinach
- 250g cow's milk ricotta
- 50g Parmesan cheese, grated
- ½ teaspoon grated nutmeg
- semolina flour, for dusting
- 75g butter
- 5 sage leaves
- salt

Start with the pasta. Put the flour in a heap on a large breadboard. Make a hole in the middle, like a volcano (in Italian the common term for this is 'a fontana' which means 'like a fountain'). Break four of the eggs into the hole and start to mix them with a fork, gradually taking in more and more flour. When you have a rough dough, start kneading with your hands – it will feel very stiff to start with, but as you continue to knead it will become smoother, softer, silkier. Knead with alternate hands, and you'll soon end up with an elongated shape – get the two ends and fold them into the middle and knead some more. Keep going until you have a smooth dough: it takes about 15 minutes and you'll know when you get there. Cover the dough with a plate and let it rest for 15 minutes.

In the meantime, wash the spinach and remove the biggest stalks. Boil it in a very little bit of water (it will release its own liquid and you don't want to lose all its goodness) until it is just wilted. Drain and gently squeeze out all of the water, then chop it finely. Put the ricotta in a small bowl and beat it lightly with a fork. Add the spinach, 15g of the grated Parmesan, the nutmeg and salt to taste – it's

better to over-season it, if anything, as you need the contrast with the smooth, bland pasta.

The next part, David does by hand with a rolling pin, turning the dough frequently, folding it and rolling it until he has a very thin, 20–25cm wide strip, which he then cuts in half lengthwise. It's harder than it sounds to get it really thin, so if you're not a natural it's easier to use a pasta machine: divide the dough into four pieces and feed each one through the machine, cycling through the settings until you get a beautiful long, thin sheet of golden pasta about 12cm wide. Lay it on a work surface very lightly dusted with semolina flour.

To make the ravioli: take one sheet of pasta dough and imagine a central line dividing it into two lengthwise. Begin to place heaped teaspoons of the filling about 2cm to the side of the imaginary central line, leaving about 5cm between each pile. Beat the remaining egg in a bowl, and paint it lightly onto the dough around each heap of filling to help seal the ravioli closed. Then fold the other side of the dough over (along that same central line) to cover the filling. Very gently, use your fingers to seal the pasta around the filling, smoothing it down and pushing out any air caught inside so they don't open up during cooking. Use a ravioli pastry cutter with a jagged edged wheel to cut out the ravioli carefully one at a time, making sure the filling is exactly in the centre of each little parcel. Repeat this process with the other sheets of pasta.

When all the ravioli are made, bring a large pan of salted water to the boil, then gently drop in the ravioli (do this in batches). They will be cooked in a couple of minutes. While they are cooking, melt the butter in a frying pan, then add the sage leaves and leave to fry gently on a low heat. Drain the ravioli, add them to the frying pan and sprinkle with the remaining Parmesan, shaking the pan to make sure they are all well-covered in butter and cheese. Serve immediately, piping hot.

SAUCES, SEASONINGS & PRESERVES

CHIMICHURRI

～

BUENOS AIRES CAFÉ

Everyone in Argentina has their own recipe for the traditional sauce, chimichurri, and everyone claims theirs is the best. The recipe below is that of Buenos Aires Café's owner Reinaldo's mum – so naturally it is the best! It is perfect with a full-blown Argentine asado (page 45), but also tastes great with fish or just as a delicious dip for fresh crusty bread.

- 1 small onion
- 1 sweet red pepper
- 1 tomato, peeled
- 1 bulb of garlic
- 3 tablespoons olive oil
- 2 tablespoons white wine vinegar
- 1 tablespoon finely chopped parsley
- 1 teaspoon finely chopped oregano
- salt
- freshly ground black pepper

Finely chop the onion, sweet red pepper and peeled tomato and put into a large bowl. Separate the garlic cloves, peel and finely chop them. Add the garlic to the bowl – yes, all of it – followed by the olive oil, vinegar, parsley and oregano. Mix it all up really well – it's important to do all this by hand and not in a blender so you get a good texture – then season to taste with salt and freshly ground black pepper.

BBQ RUB

PIG DOGS AND BRISKET

Use to season steaks, ribs and pork belly, or wherever you need a bit of BBQ wallop.

- 25g black peppercorns
- 2 teaspoons mustard seeds
- 70g white sugar
- 40g light brown sugar
- 70g salt
- 2 teaspoons chilli powder
- 1 teaspoon garlic powder
- 30g paprika
- 1 teaspoon ground ginger
- 1 teaspoon allspice powder

Grind the peppercorns and mustard seeds to a fine powder in a coffee grinder or spice mill. Combine with the white and brown sugars, salt, chilli and garlic powders, paprika, ginger and allspice. Keep in an airtight container until required.

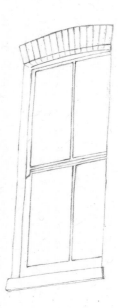

A FALSE BALANCE IS ABOMINATION TO THE LORD
BUT A JUST WEIGHT IS HIS DELIGHT

BBQ SAUCE

∾

PIG DOGS AND BRISKET

You can use this deep glossy brown sauce to make BBQ Pork Belly (page 30), Munchies' Guava BBQ Pork Tostada Mountain (page 24) and No 57A's Pulled Pork (page 28). It's tangy, sweet and spicy, keeps in the fridge for ages and is a mile better than anything you can buy in the shops. It's also very easy to make – the sieving at the end of the recipe might seem like a faff, but it's really worth doing as that's what gives you such a wonderful smooth texture.

Makes about 750ml

- 2 × 400g tins chopped tomatoes
- 500ml cider vinegar
- 250g dark brown sugar
- 6 garlic cloves, crushed
- 250ml tomato ketchup
- 2 onions, peeled and chopped
- 250ml apple juice
- 2 generous tablespoons wholegrain mustard
- 2 teaspoons English mustard powder
- 3 generous tablespoons honey
- 3 teaspoons smoked paprika
- 3 tablespoons Worcestershire sauce
- 1 tablespoon BBQ Rub (page 105)
- 1 whole red chilli
  (pick the type of chilli to suit how hot and spicy you like your sauce)
- salt
- freshly ground black pepper

Place all the ingredients apart from the salt and pepper into a large pan and bring to the boil. Once boiling, turn down to a low simmer and continue to cook for 1½ hours, stirring occasionally, until the sauce has reduced by half. Taste and season with salt and black pepper if you think it needs it.

Blitz the sauce with a stick blender or in a liquidiser and pass through a fine sieve. Leave to cool, then pour into an airtight container and keep in the refrigerator until needed.

PICKLED WATERMELON

❦

PIG DOGS AND BRISKET

This is great served with sticky BBQ pork, ribs or roast pork. You can eat it immediately once it has cooled down, though it's best after a week or two and will keep for several months.

Makes about 2 litres

- 1 medium watermelon
- 500ml cider vinegar
- 50g dark brown sugar
- 100g golden caster sugar
- 1 star anise
- 1 heaped tablespoon grated ginger
- 1 teaspoon salt

Peel the watermelon with a potato peeler – you want to remove the green skin only. Cut the watermelon into wedges and then carve out the centre of each wedge, leaving a crescent of melon rind 2–3cm thick. Cut these crescents into 2–3cm chunks and set aside.

Put the melon flesh into a food processor or liquidiser and purée until smooth, then strain through a fine sieve into a measuring jug. You need 300ml for the pickle (you'll have a lot of leftover juice, which is good: drink it with a nice gin over ice).

Place the vinegar, 300ml of the watermelon juice, the sugars, star anise, ginger and salt in a large pan and bring to the boil. Add the watermelon chunks, bring back to the boil and continue to boil for 1 minute. Remove the melon with a slotted spoon and pack into four 500ml sterilised preserving jars. Pour over the pickle juice and seal.

PICKLED CARROTS

❧

BÁNH MÌ NÊN

Simple and addictive, these Pickled Carrots are a key ingredient in all sorts of Vietnamese dishes including Tran's Bánh Mì (page 6) and Rice Noodles with Honey Lemongrass Chicken (page 11). It's worth keeping a container of them in the fridge to zest up salads and sandwiches of any kind.

- 30g sugar
- 60ml rice vinegar
- 2 carrots, cut into thin matchsticks

Mix the sugar, vinegar and 60ml hot water in a small bowl and leave at room temperature to cool right down. When the mixture is absolutely cool, add the carrots and put in the fridge for at least an hour or, ideally, overnight.

SALTED CARAMEL SAUCE

~

PLANET PANCAKE

Oh my, this is good. Not much else needs to be said. Obviously, it's terrific on pancakes but there's not much it wouldn't improve.

Makes about 350ml

• 45g unsalted butter
• 95g dark muscovado unrefined cane sugar
• 1 teaspoon extra fine iodised table salt
• 300ml extra-thick double cream

Put a small pan on a low heat, then add the butter, sugar and salt and keep stirring until the butter has melted. Add the double cream and simmer very gently for another 20 minutes, stirring all the time. Take the pan off the heat and leave it to cool.

Serve warm or cold, on pretty much anything.

RASPBERRY SAUCE

~

PLANET PANCAKE

This is another cracking sauce from the Planet Pancake boys. Sweet, tart, aromatic from all that vanilla – just lovely on ice cream, yoghurt, peaches, chocolate brownies or, of course, pancakes.

Makes about 350ml

• 350g raspberries
• 100g unrefined organic sugar
• 1½ Madagascan vanilla pod or 2½ teaspoons vanilla extract
• 1 teaspoon freshly squeezed lemon juice

Wash the raspberries in a colander and shake them dry. Put a small saucepan on a low heat, then add the raspberries, sugar and vanilla pod or extract. Cook and stir gently for about 15 minutes until the raspberries have cooked right down, then add the lemon juice and leave it to cool.

Serve warm or chilled.

"I LOVE THE DIVERSITY YOU GET HERE – BOTH AMONG THE CUSTOMERS AND THE OTHER TRADERS. YOU LEARN SOMETHING EVERY DAY, LIKE A NEW IDEA FOR THE BUSINESS OR A NEW FLAVOUR TO TRY. IT KEEPS MY MIND MOVING."

Neil, *Planet Pancake*

BLACKBERRY JAM

❧

BONBON CAFÉ

This is Grace's favourite jam to make and eat, both because of its amazing flavour and because it reminds her of her childhood in Berkshire. It was the first jam she made as a teenager and is a great place for anyone to start, not least because you can get the blackberries for free if you know the right hedgerow. Blackberries are very low in pectin, so the addition of apples and lemon juice is crucial to help the jam set, as well as rounding out the flavour. Delicious on toast or with some good strong cheese.

Makes about 3kg

- 675g cooking apples
- juice and zest of 1 lemon
- 1.35kg blackberries
- 2kg sugar (if the blackberries are very sweet, reduce this to 1.8kg)
- 50g fresh ginger, grated

Cut the apples into small pieces (don't peel or core them first). Put them in a saucepan with the lemon juice, then add 500ml water and bring to the boil. Simmer until soft, then push the contents of the pan through a sieve with a wooden spoon (making sure you get as much of the pulp through as possible).

Put the blackberries in a large, heavy-bottomed saucepan and mix in the apple purée, sugar, lemon zest and ginger. Heat slowly, stirring until the sugar dissolves. Increase the heat and boil to jam setting point – 104°C/220°F on a sugar thermometer. This should take about 20 minutes. If you have no thermometer, use the plate test – put a little jam on a plate or saucer and let it cool. If it wrinkles when you push it with a finger, it's ready.

Take the pan off the heat and let it cool for 15 minutes. Skim off any scum that's gathered on the top, then stir and pour into six 500ml hot, sterilised jars, seal and label.

SWEET THINGS AND DRINKS

BACIO GELATO

❧

BLACK VANILLA

All Italians know that the legendary flavour combination of cocoa and hazelnut was invented in the mountainous north-west region of Italy – and thanks to a very successful little jar of spread containing the two ingredients, it's a combination that is world famous.

Black Vanilla's perfectly creamy, delicious *Bacio Gelato* celebrates that perfect match: *bacio* is Italian for kiss – which explains why you'll keep going back for more... Kids, obviously, go crazy for it.

Serves 6

- 330ml whole milk
- 100g caster sugar
- 10g cocoa powder
- 170ml double cream
- 50g hazelnuts

Put the milk, sugar and cocoa powder in a saucepan over a low heat. Keep stirring until the sugar has dissolved and the cocoa is fully mixed in; make sure it doesn't come to the boil. Take the pan off the heat and add the double cream. Give it a good stir and churn in an ice-cream machine for 30–40 minutes (or freeze for 4 hours, stirring with a fork every 30 minutes).

While the gelato is freezing, lightly roast the hazelnuts on a baking tray in the oven at 170ºC. They should be done in about 15–20 minutes, but give them a shake after 10 minutes to stop them burning. Rub their skins off, then roughly chop.

When your gelato is ready, fold in the hazelnuts, saving a handful to scatter on top.

YOGHURT GELATO

❧

BLACK VANILLA

This contains only four per cent fat, freezes really fast and is absolutely wonderful: tangy, creamy and light. You could use a fat-free yoghurt but the resulting gelato will be harder and, of course, less tasty.

Serves 6

- 300g plain yoghurt
- 150g whole milk
- 95g caster sugar
- fresh fruit or chocolate chips (optional)

Mix the yoghurt, milk and sugar with a stick blender until the sugar is dissolved and... that's it! Pour into your ice-cream machine and churn for 25 minutes or so, or put in a freezer-proof container in the deep freeze for about 4 hours, stirring with a fork every 20–30 minutes. Add fresh fruit or chocolate chips (or anything you like really) at the end of churning or as a topping.

VEGAN COCONUT STRACCIATELLA

BLACK VANILLA

The most difficult bit in this recipe is pronouncing the word stracciatella (which means 'a little shred'). Black Vanilla highly recommend you use fresh Thai coconuts, easy to find in good fruit shops or online – they have much more coconut water than regular brown coconuts and the flesh is more like a firm jelly. If you can't find them, use coconut milk or coconut purée (but make sure the fat content is between 15 and 20 per cent – it will say on the tin). You can use white caster sugar to keep the gelato a brilliant white, or muscovado sugar for deeper toffee overtones.

Serves 6

- 200g young coconut meat (or 265ml coconut milk)
- 220ml coconut water (or 160ml if you're making this with coconut milk)
- 85g caster or muscovado sugar
- 40g dark chocolate chips

Mix the coconut meat and water with the sugar in a food processor and blend as much as possible. If you're using coconut milk this is so easy – just mix with a stick blender until the sugar has dissolved. Pour into your ice-cream machine and churn for 30–40 minutes or so (or freeze for 4 hours, stirring with a fork every 20–30 minutes). When your gelato is ready, fold in your 'little shreds' of chocolate and enjoy.

SORBETTO ALLA PESCA

(Peach Sorbet)

❧

BLACK VANILLA

There's nothing like the smell and the sweetness of a good ripe peach, especially on a hot summer's day. This beautiful dusky rose-coloured sorbet captures that full floral flavour and is so smooth and creamy that it is hard to believe it is fat free.

It is also incredibly easy to make – you don't have to bother peeling the peaches but if you prefer to, go ahead. The sugar quantities indicated are a guideline only – if you have very sweet peaches, use a little less of the syrup.

Serves 6

• 100g caster sugar
• 400g peaches

Put the sugar and 100ml water in a small saucepan and bring to the boil. Simmer for 3 minutes until you have a light syrup, then leave it to cool.

Wash the peaches, cut them in half and remove all the stones. Put them in a bowl, add the cool sugar syrup and blend with a stick blender until smooth. Churn for 30–40 minutes in an ice-cream machine (or freeze for 4 hours, stirring with a fork every 30 minutes) and enjoy...

P.S. This is a killer ingredient for your cocktails! Try it in a Bellini: put a scoop in the bottom of a glass and top up with Champagne.

RASPBERRY AND VANILLA CHEESECAKE

LILIKA'S TREATS

This is lovely – a summer treat and a great way to use the first of the season's rasps. It's rich and creamy, with a gingery, salty base, all offset by a tart fresh raspberry purée. Be warned, it's very moreish.

Serves 10

- 50g whole unblanched almonds
- 200g ginger biscuits
- 80g salted butter
- 300g caster sugar
- 600g full-fat cream cheese
- 1 vanilla pod
- 2 eggs, lightly beaten
- 50g plain flour
- 80g raspberries
- 1 tablespoon honey

Preheat the oven to 190ºC. In a food processor, blitz the almonds and ginger biscuits until they turn into fine crumbs. Melt the butter in a saucepan and add it little by little to the crumb mixture until it has the consistency of wet sand. You might not need all the butter, or you might need a little more – if it still looks a bit dry, melt another 20g of butter and add it bit by bit until the crumbs stick together. Press the mixture evenly into the bottom of a 30cm springform cake tin using your hands or the back of a spoon, making sure you don't leave any gaps.

Put the tin in the oven and bake for 10 minutes or so until the base is golden brown. Remove to a wire rack to cool and turn the oven temperature down to 160ºC.

While the base is in the oven, cream the caster sugar and cream cheese together with an electric mixer until all the sugar is blended in perfectly. Cut the vanilla pod in half lengthwise and scrape in the seeds, then add the eggs and mix for a further 60 seconds. Finally, sift in the flour and gently whisk it into the batter with a balloon whisk.

In a separate bowl, crush the raspberries and honey together – a stick blender gives it a fine, runny consistency which makes it easy to pour onto the cheesecake. If you don't like the seeds, you could always sieve the raspberries – it's up to you. Put the resulting purée in a jug or a piping bag to make it easier to use later.

Scrape all the cheesecake batter onto the cooled base and even out the surface with a spatula. Then pipe or pour the raspberry purée onto the cheesecake – Elika usually makes a spiral pattern starting from the middle of the tin and then makes lines from the centre of the spiral outwards using a table knife – but you could do swirls, heart shapes, even dots: whatever you like. Put the cheesecake in the oven and bake for 30 minutes or until the edges start to set. It will seem a bit wobbly when you take it out of the oven but it really firms up on cooling.

Once the cheesecake has completely cooled, chill overnight in the fridge before serving. Don't put it in the fridge before it is completely cold or cracks might form on the top, messing up your beautiful raspberry pattern.

SAFFRON RICE PUDDING

∼

MOGUL

This traditional saffron-scented Indian rice pudding owes its particular richness to the inclusion of whole milk, which is reduced by more than half during the cooking process to make a thick, creamy base. Sweet, comforting and aromatic, this is delicious served in little bowls either straight from the pan or chilled.

Serves 4

• 50g basmati rice
• 15g unsalted butter
• ½ teaspoon lightly crushed saffron threads
• ½ teaspoon ground cardamom
• 600ml whole milk
• 100ml single cream
• 150g caster sugar
• 20g flaked almonds
• 20g pistachios, thinly sliced
• 3–4 drops rose water

Rinse the rice under running water until the water runs clear and then drain it thoroughly.

Melt the butter over a medium heat in a large heavy-bottomed saucepan and add the drained rice, saffron and cardamom. Fry, stirring gently, for about 2 minutes until you can smell the spices. Pour in the milk and cream and cook, stirring occasionally, for about 1 hour until the milk is reduced by half and the rice is tender. You may need to turn the heat down as the milk reduces.

Add the sugar, almonds and half of the pistachios and stir over a medium-low heat until the sugar dissolves (about 2 minutes). Transfer to individual serving bowls, and garnish with the remaining pistachios and the rose water before serving.

CHOCOLATE FINANCIERS

~∾~

SAINT SUGAR OF LONDON

A financier is a little almond cake, maybe not as famous as a madeleine outside France, but for Enzo of Saint Sugar of London it's the real deal. According to legend, it was created by a pastry chef in a pâtisserie close to the Paris Stock Exchange in the second half of the 19th century. As its name suggests, it was made as an homage to the bankers and has the traditional shape of a little gold bar.

Any serious pastry shop in Paris sells financiers, even if nowadays they are often made as a bigger muffin-shaped version. They are characterised by the use of ground almonds, egg white, *beurre noisette* (brown butter) and icing sugar. Many gluten-free baked goods dry out very quickly, but Saint Sugar's take on this French pâtisserie classic is extremely moist and dense, and absolutely delicious. This is a really useful recipe whether or not you can eat gluten – very quick to make, and the cakes will keep in an airtight container for up to two weeks. They look very plain, but they taste absolutely wonderful.

Makes 10

- 85g unsalted butter
- 2 egg whites
- 130g ground almonds
- 100g icing sugar
- 4 tablespoons cocoa powder
- ½ teaspoon salt
- ¼ teaspoon almond extract

Preheat the oven to 190°C. Gently melt the butter in a small pan over a low heat until it browns. In a large bowl, lightly beat the egg whites with a fork, then fold in the ground almonds, icing sugar, cocoa powder and salt. Stir in the melted brown butter and almond extract and mix until you have a smooth batter.

Put a heaped tablespoon of the batter into each cavity of a 10-hole financier mould (or use mini-loaf moulds) and bake in the oven for 10–15 minutes.

Cool on a wire rack before turning out.

PLEIN ARÔME

~

SAINT SUGAR OF LONDON

Saint Sugar of London never hold back on the flavour front as this fantastic gluten-free, dairy-free and sugar-free chocolate loaf demonstrates. *Plein Arôme* (full flavour!) is a rich and complex bit of cakery: damp and heavy with cocoa and ground almonds, aromatic, bitter, sweet – it's all there. They subtitle it 'chocolate slice' but that's really underselling its charms.

Enzo says: 'There is a big trend for free-from baked goods in London. People are more aware of allergies and are increasingly health conscious. Guilt-free treats are fashionable. This chocolate cake is a big hit with the young crowds.' And unlike many sugar-free cakes and sweets found commercially, it contains no chemical storm of sugar alternatives: all the sweetness comes from natural dried fruit. You'll get a sweeter finish if you use dates, whereas prunes give a more rounded, complex flavour.

Makes 1 large loaf

- 350g pitted dates or pitted prunes
- 3 eggs
- 2 tablespoons coconut oil
- 2 teaspoons vanilla extract
- 350g ground almonds
- 120g cocoa powder
- ½ teaspoon bicarbonate of soda
- pinch of salt

Preheat the oven to 190ºC. Grease and line a 900g loaf tin.

In a food processor, blend the dates with 120ml water until you have a smooth paste. Transfer the date paste to a large bowl and mix with the eggs, coconut oil and vanilla extract. In another bowl, stir together all the dry ingredients: the ground almonds, cocoa, bicarbonate of soda and salt. Add the dry ingredients to the wet and beat until smooth, adding 250ml water until you have a thick but pourable batter. Pour into your prepared tin, level off the top and bake in the oven for 40–45 minutes or until a skewer inserted in the middle comes out clean.

Let the cake cool in the tin on a wire rack for few hours, before turning out and serving in delicious guilt-free slices.

FONDANTS AU CHOCOLAT

ઌ

CHAMPAGNE + FROMAGE

This is one of Champagne + Fromage's signature recipes – a super simple and very elegant chocolate fondant, given a twist with the addition of a hidden blue-cheese centre.

Before you raise your eyebrows in horror, just try it – the Champagne + Fromage crew know what they're about. The cheese adds a little saltiness and a mouth-filling ripeness that work wonderfully with good dark chocolate. They use a ewe's milk cheese called *Bleu des Basques,* which is creamy and sharp at the same – if you have trouble getting hold of it, try any blue cheese that's not too strong. The recipe doubles up really easily so it makes a sophisticated pudding option for dinner parties.

Serves 5

- 100g 70 per cent dark chocolate, broken into squares
- 100g butter, diced
- 2 eggs
- 2 egg yolks
- 100g golden caster sugar
- 100g plain flour, sifted
- 30g *Bleu des Basques* cheese, cut into 5 even pieces
- icing sugar, for dusting

Preheat the oven to 220ºC.

Put the chocolate and butter in a bowl over a pan of barely simmering water, and slowly melt them together. Remove the bowl from the heat and stir gently until smooth and glossy, then leave to cool for about 10 minutes.

In a separate bowl, whisk the whole eggs and yolks together with the sugar until the mixture is pale and thick, and the whisk leaves a trail for a few seconds when you lift it. Beat in the flour. Pour the melted chocolate into the egg mixture in thirds, beating well between each addition, until it is all combined and you have a loose, homogenous batter.

Put five 7cm baking tins or ceramic ramekins on a baking tray. Half fill each of them with the batter – you might find it easiest to put the batter into a wide-ended icing bag to do this – then pop a piece of cheese on top. Fill the tins with the remaining batter and put in the oven for 12 minutes. Dust with icing sugar to serve.

CHOCOLATE CHIP HAZELNUT BANANA BREAD

❧

RUBYS OF LONDON

Ruby's wonderfully decadent vegan baking is a revelation whether you are vegan or not. Her take on banana bread is dairy-free, egg-free, wheat-free, gluten-free, refined-sugar-free but very definitely not pleasure-free – it will make a lot of people with dietary restrictions very happy indeed. Mini loaves are now much easier to make thanks to the paper moulds you can buy in any cookshop – it's well worth hunting them out.

Makes 14 mini loaves or 1 large loaf

- 325g gluten-free flour
- 35g ground almonds
- 2 teaspoons gluten-free baking powder
- 2 teaspoons bicarbonate of soda
- 1 teaspoon xanthum gum
- 1 teaspoon cinnamon
- 120ml sunflower oil
- 250ml agave nectar (or any natural liquid sweetener you prefer)
- 225ml unsweetened dairy-free milk (Ruby likes to use almond milk)
- 2 teaspoons vanilla extract
- 500g mashed ripe banana (about 4 small bananas)
- 85g unsweetened apple purée
- 150g 70 per cent best quality dark chocolate, roughly chopped (Ruby uses Montezuma's)
- 50g roasted hazelnuts, chopped

Preheat the oven to 170ºC. If you're using paper loaf moulds, arrange them on a baking tray. If you're using loaf tins, lightly grease them.

Sift together the gluten-free flour, ground almonds, baking powder, bicarbonate of soda, xanthum gum and cinnamon into a large bowl. In another larger bowl, whisk together the oil, agave nectar, dairy-free milk and vanilla extract. Add the dry ingredients to the wet and gently fold in until everything is well combined. Add the mashed banana, apple purée, chocolate chips and hazelnuts and continue to fold gently so you have a thickish batter. If you're making mini loaves, spread the batter equally between the moulds using an ice-cream scoop or a spoon. Otherwise, scrape it into your loaf tin and level off the top.

Bake in the oven for 25–30 minutes for mini loaves, or 1¼ hours for the large loaf. They are done when a skewer inserted into the middle comes out clean. Cool in the tins on a wire rack before turning out. The cakes will keep for 2 to 3 days wrapped in clingfilm in an airtight tin.

CHOCOLATE CHIP COOKIES

~

GREENWICH COOKIE TIME

Tom's chocolate chip cookies are absolute classics. Chewy, soft, sweet and also just ever so slightly salty, they're a cinch to make and won't clutter up your kitchen for long once they're out of the oven. Delicious.

Makes 10 cookies

- 150g plain flour
- small pinch bicarbonate of soda
- ½ teaspoon salt
- small pinch ground nutmeg
- 100g butter, softened
- 140g light soft brown sugar
- 20g caster sugar
- ¼ teaspoon vanilla extract
- 1 medium egg
- 150g milk chocolate chips

Preheat the oven to 180°C. Line two large baking trays with baking parchment.

Sift the flour into a bowl and add the bicarbonate of soda, salt and nutmeg. In a separate bowl, cream the butter, both the sugars and the vanilla extract together until light and fluffy – it's easiest to do this with an electric mixer. Add the egg and mix again, scraping down the sides of the bowl to make sure you've got every last bit. Fold in the flour and chocolate chips to form a dryish dough. Divide the dough into 10 equal pieces, then roll each one into a ball and flatten slightly with the palm of your hands. Place the dough balls on your prepared trays, allowing plenty of space between them as they will spread quite a lot in the oven. Bake for 10–12 minutes until they are golden brown and start to crisp on the edges, remembering to turn the tray 180 degrees halfway through the bake for an even colour.

Let the cookies cool on the tray for 5 minutes, then transfer them to a wire rack to cool completely before eating. Store the cookies in an airtight container – they will keep well for at least 2 days.

VANILLA SHORTBREAD

❧

GREENWICH COOKIE TIME

Tender-crumbed and flecked with vanilla, these are wonderful and rather elegant little biscuits. The unbaked dough will hold in the fridge for up to 10 days, so you can bake a few whenever you fancy with no hassle at all.

Makes about 30 small cookies or 10 large cookies

- 100g unsalted butter, softened
- 50g caster sugar
- ½ vanilla pod
- 100g plain flour
- 50g cornflour
- small pinch of salt

Cream the butter and sugar together with an electric mixer until light and well combined. Scrape the seeds out of the vanilla pod and add them to the mixture along with the flours and salt. Mix on a low speed to form a stiff, dry dough. Roll the dough into a log of about 3cm in diameter for small biscuits, 6cm for larger ones. Wrap this in some clingfilm and put it in the fridge for at least an hour to firm up.

When you're ready to make your shortbread, preheat the oven to 160°C and line a couple of baking trays with baking parchment. Take the dough log out of the fridge and slice into discs 1cm thick. Arrange on the prepared trays and bake until they are the lightest gold – small biscuits will take 18–20 minutes, larger biscuits will take 24–25 minutes. Turn the baking trays 180 degrees halfway through the bake for an even colour. Cool on a wire tray and enjoy.

Store the biscuits in an airtight container for up to a week.

COCONUT COOKIES

⤜∾⤛

GREENWICH COOKIE TIME

Another great recipe from Tom at Greenwich Cookie Time – the dough is delicious before it even goes near an oven, and the finished biscuits are even better. Even coconut haters might well find themselves snaffling a few of these.

Makes 12 cookies

- 180g plain flour
- ¼ teaspoon baking powder
- ¼ teaspoon bicarbonate of soda
- ½ teaspoon salt
- 90g desiccated coconut
- 100g unsalted butter, softened

- 85g caster sugar
- 85g light soft brown sugar
- ½ teaspoon vanilla extract
- 1 small egg
- 1 large egg yolk

Preheat the oven to 180°C and line two baking trays with baking parchment.

Sift the flour into a bowl and add the baking powder, bicarbonate of soda, salt and desiccated coconut. In an electric mixer, cream together the butter, both sugars and the vanilla extract until they are light and fluffy. Add the egg, making sure it's well mixed in and scraping down the sides of the bowl, then add the egg yolk and mix again until it's thoroughly combined and has a moussey consistency. Fold in the dry ingredients and bring together to make a soft dough.

Divide the dough into 12 equal pieces and roll each one into a ball. Flatten each ball slightly between the palm of your hands and put on the prepared baking trays, leaving space between them as they will spread in the oven. Bake for about 10–12 minutes until they are a deep golden brown, turning the trays 180 degrees halfway through the bake for an even colour. Let the cookies cool completely on a wire rack before eating.

Store the biscuits in an airtight container; they will keep well for at least 3 days.

SCONES

❧

RED DOOR CAFÉ

Kate and Suzanne at the lovely Red Door Café were a bit reticent about handing over their scone recipe, not because it was a closely guarded secret, but because, as Kate says: 'I taught Suzanne how to do it, but neither of us really has a recipe as such and are more chuck-in-a-bit-of-this-and-that type cooks. And scones are strange and some days they seem to come out lovely and other days not. Compared to other recipes, we definitely use more sugar and butter, but hey, that's what makes things taste good, isn't it?' Well, they make terrific scones and this basic recipe is a winner. You could add raisins or vanilla extract or ground almonds, and if you like cheese scones just leave out the sugar and add some good quality Cheddar, grated, once you've rubbed in the butter.

Makes about 10 scones

- 250g self-raising flour
- 75g caster sugar
- 100g salted butter, softened
- 150ml whole milk (though you may well need less)

Preheat your oven to at least 220°C – it needs to be really hot. Have a baking tray ready and covered with a sheet of baking paper.

Mix together the flour and sugar in a large bowl. Dice the butter, then rub it into the flour mixture with your fingertips until it resembles breadcrumbs and all the butter is rubbed in. If the mixture holds together in a clump when you squeeze it then you know it has enough butter in there. If it's too powdery then you could add a bit more butter.

Add half the milk and quickly stir it in. You want a firm dough that sticks together – add a splash more of the milk if it's too dry, and if it gets too wet add a bit more flour. Don't play with the dough too much and don't hang about or leave it out for long: you want to get it in the oven quickly. Put the dough onto a floured work surface and press it into a round about 2cm thick. Cut out your scones with a 5cm cutter or upturned glass and place them on the baking tray. Brush with milk and bake in the oven for 10–15 minutes, checking frequently – you may have to turn the tray halfway through to get even cooking depending on your oven and its hot spots.

When the scones are golden and risen, take them out and dust with a little flour before leaving them to cool slightly on a wire rack. Kate recommends serving the scones while still warm, spread first with good-quality strawberry jam and then an enormous pile of clotted cream.

SPICED WALNUT CAKE

❧

ARAPINA

This is a lovely Greek cake which happens to be free from dairy and gluten – it has a nubbly texture and a rich flavour from the walnuts, and it is soaked in a fragrant lemon-cinnamon syrup which makes it moist and sweet. Cut into neat diamonds it makes an indulgent treat – and it also keeps for ages. Michaela also makes a reduced-sugar version: she cuts the sugar in the cake down to 200g and uses 10g of stevia instead of sugar to make the syrup (following the same method as below).

Serves 12–15

for the cake:
- 370ml olive oil
- 250g caster sugar
- 5 eggs
- juice and zest of 1 orange
- juice and zest of 1 lemon
- 1 teaspoon gluten-free baking powder
- 1½ teaspoons bicarbonate of soda
- ½ teaspoon vanilla extract
- ½ teaspoon ground cinnamon
- ½ teaspoon ground cloves
- 300g gluten-free plain flour
- 150g walnuts, chopped

for the syrup:
- 100g caster sugar
- 1 lemon, halved
- 2 cinnamon sticks

Preheat the oven to 170°C and grease and line a 32 x 20cm brownie tin.

The cake is easiest to make with an electric mixer, but you can also do it with a wooden spoon and a strong arm. Put the oil and sugar in a large bowl and beat until thick and syrupy. With the mixer still running, add the eggs one by one and continue to beat. Put the orange and lemon juice in a small bowl, then add the baking powder and bicarbonate of soda and stir to dissolve. Stir it into the batter. When it's fully mixed in, add the vanilla, orange and lemon zest, cinnamon and cloves and then finally the flour and the walnuts. Scrape the batter into your prepared tin and bake for 35–40 minutes until a skewer pushed into the middle of the cake comes out clean and dry. Let the cake cool in the tin on a wire rack while you make the syrup.

Put the sugar, lemon halves and cinnamon sticks into a small pan with 100ml water and simmer for 12–15 minutes. Strain the lightly scented syrup into a jug and pour over the cool cake. Cut the cake into diamond shapes to serve.

KALLITSOUNIA

❧❧❧

ARAPINA

Kallitsounia come from Crete, and are rather like individual cheesecakes subtly flavoured with mint and cinnamon on a sweet pastry crust.

Traditionally they are made to be eaten on Easter Sunday to celebrate the end of the long Lenten fast – sweet enough to be celebratory, light enough to re-accustom your body to eating dairy and eggs after a period of abstinence. They are absolutely delicious. In Crete, they would use a soft white cheese called *mizithra* for the filling – it's not widely available in the UK so, unless you're lucky enough to have a Greek deli nearby, use ricotta instead. You can also try them without any sugar in the filling, for a more savoury and sweet combination.

Makes about 20

for the pastry:
- 125ml milk
- 1 teaspoon baking powder
- ¼ teaspoon vanilla extract
- 125ml olive oil
- 125ml sunflower oil
- 90g soft brown sugar
- 1 egg
- 250–350g plain flour

for the filling:
- 500g *mizithra* or ricotta
- 65g caster sugar
- 1 egg
- 3 mint leaves, finely chopped
- ½ teaspoon cinnamon powder

for the topping:
- 1 egg, beaten
- ½ teaspoon cinnamon powder

Preheat the oven to 160ºC and then get started on the pastry.

Warm the milk slightly in a small saucepan. Stir in the baking powder and vanilla extract and take off the heat. . Put the olive oil and sunflower oil in the bowl of an electric mixer and beat in the sugar. Then, with the mixer still running, add the egg and the milk mixture and keep beating until thoroughly mixed. Swap the mixer for your hands and slowly add the flour, starting with 250g and adding more until the dough leaves the sides of the bowl clean. Keep working it until you have a lovely soft, oily dough. Flour your worktop and roll out the dough to about 7mm, then cut out as many 8cm rounds as you can. Gather up the scraps and repeat – you should get about 20.

Quickly make the filling – put the ricotta, sugar, egg, mint and cinnamon in a bowl and beat well with a fork.

Take a scant tablespoon of the filling mixture and put it in the centre of one of the pastry rounds. Put the round in the palm of your left hand, and with your other hand make pleats all around the edge of the pastry, pinching them tightly to form a raised rim around the filling. Traditionally, they would be baked like this, but as the dough is so soft you might want to put them in jam tart tins to help hold the rim in place. Once all the *kallitsounia* are made, brush lightly with beaten egg and sprinkle a little cinnamon powder on the top.

Bake in the oven for 30–35 minutes until golden brown, then cool on a wire rack.

THE GREENWICH MARKET COOKBOOK

MELOMAKARONA

(Honey Christmas Cookies)

❧

ARAPINA

This is a classic Greek recipe traditionally made just before Christmas – the name actually means 'pasta made out of honey'. As Michaela says, it is very apt for the festive season because it has a little present inside: a walnut half is inserted into the dough, then the whole lot is soaked in a cinnamon-infused honey syrup after cooking. By all means use stevia to make the syrup – instead of the sugar use 5g stevia, increase the honey to 6 tablespoons, and proceed as per the recipe below.

Makes about 10

for the cookies:
- 125ml olive oil
- 25g caster sugar
- 1 tablespoon Cognac
- 3 tablespoons orange juice
- ½ teaspoon baking powder
- 250g plain flour

- 10 walnut halves, plusmore to garnish
- ground cinnamon, for dusting (optional)

for the syrup:
- 30g caster sugar
- 4½ tablespoons honey
- 1 cinnamon stick

Preheat the oven to 160°C and grease a large baking tray.

Put the oil and sugar in a large bowl and beat to a glossy syrup with an electric mixer. In a small jug, mix the Cognac, orange juice and baking powder together, then add to the oil and sugar mixture and continue to beat. Put aside the mixer and use your hands to knead in the flour – don't overwork it, just mix until you have a soft dough. Add a bit more oil if it's too firm, or a bit more flour if it's too soft.

Take a handful of the dough and shape it into an oval about 8cm long, 3cm wide and 2cm thick. Make a depression in the top, push in a walnut half then pinch the dough over the top to fully cover it. Repeat with all the remaining dough, then put the cookies on the prepared baking tray and bake in the oven for 20–30 minutes until they are golden brown.

Meanwhile, prepare the honey syrup. Put the sugar, honey and cinnamon stick in a small pan with 100ml water and bring to the boil. Skim off any foam that forms on the surface and simmer for 15 minutes or so, then leave to cool for 5 minutes. As soon as the *melomakarona* come out of the oven, drop them into the warm syrup and leave them to soak for 10 minutes. Remove to a beautiful plate and sprinkle with some more walnuts, finely chopped, and maybe a little ground cinnamon.

KOURAMPIEDES

∽

ARAPINA

These little almond pastries are another Christmas delicacy from Greece, usually made just before Christmas day in enormous quantities then kept in airtight containers to see the family through the festive season. Star or heart-shaped and dredged in a thick layer of icing sugar, they really look the part and are incredibly moreish and delicious.

Makes about 30

- 65g blanched almonds, roughly chopped
- 250g unsalted butter (or fresh-milk Corfu butter if you can get it), softened
- 60g caster sugar
- 1 egg yolk
- 2 tablespoons Cognac, plus more for sprinkling
- 2 tablespoons ground cinnamon
- 250g plain flour
- 125g icing sugar

Preheat the oven to 200°C and grease a baking tray.

Put the almonds on a separate baking tray, sprinkle with a little water and roast in the oven until they are light brown, then set aside to cool. Turn the oven down to 160°C.

Put the butter and sugar in a large bowl and use an electric mixer to cream them together until very pale and light. Add the egg yolk and Cognac and beat again until very thoroughly combined, then beat in the cinnamon. With your hands now, mix in the roasted almonds and then, little by little, the flour until you have a soft but workable dough.

Either roll out the dough and stamp out hearts or stars, or take walnut-sized pieces of the dough and make into round cookies as you like. Put them on the prepared baking tray and bake in the oven for 20–25 minutes until the biscuits are the lightest golden brown. Cool on a wire rack, then sprinkle with some more Cognac. Dredge with a festively thick layer of icing sugar.

SARAGLI

(Sweet Filo Pastry)

୭୭

ARAPINA

This is another of Michaela's wonderful family recipes, marking very clearly their journey from Asia Minor (on the south-west coast of Turkey) to Crete. Filo pastry, almonds and walnuts all soaked in syrup – it's a super-sweet dessert that has very strong Turkish influences, but has become part of the Cretan culinary culture. Increasingly, Michaela uses stevia instead of sugar in her syrups – if you want to try this, substitute 25g of stevia for the sugar and add four tablespoons of honey.

Enjoy with a small cup of very strong coffee to cut through the sweetness.

Makes about 30

- 100g almonds, chopped
- 100g walnuts, chopped
- 25g breadcrumbs
- ½ teaspoon ground cloves
- ½ teaspoon ground cinnamon
- 125g unsalted butter
  (or Corfu fresh-milk butter
  if you can find it)
- 250g filo pastry

for the syrup:
- 250g caster sugar
- ½ tablespoon freshly squeezed
  lemon juice

Preheat the oven to 200ºC. Put the almonds on a baking tray and roast in the oven for 10 minutes until golden brown. Put them in a large bowl with the walnuts, breadcrumbs and spices and mix thoroughly with your hands. Turn the oven down to 180ºC.

Melt the butter in a small pan over a low heat. Put a piece of filo pastry on the table with the longest side nearest you and brush it liberally with melted butter. Put another piece of filo on top and brush with more butter, then cover with a very thin layer of the nut mixture. Be careful that it doesn't spill over the edges. Roll up the pastry from the edge nearest to you – not so loose that the filling comes out, and not so tight that the filo tears. Push the ends of the roll in gently so the whole thing concertinas very slightly, then cut it into pieces about 5cm long. Repeat with all the remaining filo sheets, then brush the inside of a deep baking tray with lots more melted butter and put all the *saragli* neatly inside. Bake for about 25 minutes until golden brown and crispy.

While the *saragli* are baking, make the syrup. Put the sugar and lemon juice into a pan with 125ml water and bring to the boil. Keep stirring until the sugar dissolves, then simmer for about 10 minutes to thicken. Pour over enough syrup to come about two-thirds of the way up the *saragli,* then leave for 3 hours or so to let the pastries soak it up. Remove from the tin to serve: the tops will be crispy and the bottoms soft and syrupy – utterly delicious.

"I SELL FRESH MACARONS AND I PUT MY HEART AND SOUL INTO MAKING THEM. I LIKE EVERYTHING ABOUT THE MARKET. THE PEOPLE, THE FOOD, THE VIBE, THE TRADERS, ABSOLUTELY EVERYTHING. NEVER BEFORE HAVE I EXPERIENCED A PLACE SO FULL OF POSITIVE ENERGY – IT'S IN A GREAT LOCATION, THE MARKET IS BEAUTIFUL, AND EVERYONE WHO STEPS IN IS WONDERFUL, LOCALS AND TOURISTS ALIKE."

Elika, *Lilika's Treats*

TSOUREKAKIA

(Easter Cookies)

ᘓᘐᘓ

ARAPINA

These are an Easter treat originating, like many of Michaela's recipes, from the Greek communities in Asia Minor. They are dairy-free, and so were traditionally eaten while people were fasting in the 40 days leading up to Easter. Unlike a lot of Greek sweets, they don't come drenched in syrup and are particularly nice dipped in strong coffee. Sometimes Michaela makes them with wholemeal flour – it's up to you, try them both ways!

Makes 35–40

- 300g vegetable fat spread (eg. Stork or Vitalite)
- 240g caster sugar
- 1 small egg plus 1 egg yolk
- 1 teaspoon baking powder
- ¼ teaspoon bicarbonate of soda
- 1 tablespoon brandy
- ¼ teaspoon vanilla extract
- 160ml orange juice
- 500g plain flour

Preheat the oven to 170ºC and grease two large baking trays.

Put the vegetable spread and sugar in a large bowl and cream together with an electric mixer until really light and fluffy. Beat the egg, and add about half of it to the bowl along with the egg yolk, and then beat again until you have a pale, moussey mixture. Stir the baking powder, bicarbonate of soda, brandy and vanilla extract into the orange juice, then pour into the mixture while the mixer is running and beat once again until fully incorporated. With your hands now, incorporate the flour to make a soft but workable dough. You may need a little more flour – see how it feels.

Take small handfuls of the dough and roll into ropes about 10cm long and 1.5cm in diameter. Pick them up in the middle and wind the ends around each other to form a simple twist shape, then put on the prepared baking trays. If the dough is too soft to form into shapes, you can go freestyle and drop spoonfuls directly onto the baking trays. Brush lightly with the leftover beaten egg and bake in the oven for 20 minutes or so until golden brown. Cool on a wire rack before serving.

BLACKBERRY LAVENDER RAW CAKE

ARAPINA

This is an utterly guilt free treat: pretty as a picture, gluten-free, dairy-free, sugar-free, vegan, full of raw power and absolutely delicious.

Serves 8

for the base:
- 240g brazil nuts
- 160g pitted dates
- 100g shredded coconut
- 4 teaspoons coconut oil

for the banana cashew cream;
- 6 ripe bananas
- 150g raw cashew nuts, soaked in water for 2 hours
- 250ml coconut water
- 4 fresh lavender leaves

for the blackberry lavender layer:
- 4 ripe bananas

- 70g blackberries
- 4 fresh lavender leaves
- 1 tablespoon lecithin granules
- 3 pitted dates

for the blackberry coulis:
- 350g blackberries
- 260g pitted dates
- 1 tablespoon lecithin granules
- 1 tablespoon psyllium seed husks
- 150ml coconut water
- dried edible rose petals to garnish

Start with the base. Put the brazil nuts, dates, coconut and coconut oil in a food processor and blend until you have a thick paste. Scrape this out into a 20cm springform cake tin and press it into the base in an even layer.

Next make the banana cashew cream. Peel the bananas and put into the food processor with the drained cashew nuts, coconut water and lavender leaves. Pulse until you have a smooth, creamy texture. Pour this evenly on top of the date base.

Make the blackberry lavender layer next. Peel the bananas and process them with the blackberries, the lavender leaves, lecithin granules and pitted dates. Pulse until smooth and spread carefully onto the cake.

Finally, put the coulis ingredients – blackberries, dates, lecithin granules, psyllium seed husks and coconut water – in the food processor and blend until smooth. Use this to make a final layer on the top of the cake, then put it in the fridge and leave overnight to chill.

When you're ready to serve, take the cake from the fridge and carefully remove the springform (you might need to ease a knife around the edges first). Slice and serve immediately, artfully sprinkled with dried rose petals.

CHOCOLATE AND ALMOND PROTEIN BALLS

᷅

ARAPINA

These little beauties are vegan-friendly and free from gluten and refined sugar – full instead of natural, slow-release energy and nutritional goodness – perfect for a mid-afternoon pick-me-up. They are really popular on Arapina's weekend stall, providing hordes of health-conscious shoppers with a much needed energy boost, and would make a valuable addition to any lunchbox. They are a doddle to make and keep well in the fridge so you could make a batch on a Sunday to see you through the week.

Makes 35–40

- 2 tablespoons stevia
- 250g pitted dates
- 6 tablespoons coconut oil
- 80g cocoa butter
- 300g desiccated coconut flakes
- 160g raw cacao powder
- 300g ground almonds
- 50g flaked almonds, roughly chopped
- sea salt

Put the stevia, dates, coconut oil, cocoa butter, coconut flakes, cacao powder and ground almonds in a food processor with three or so pinches of sea salt. Blitz until you have a paste, then turn the mixture out into a bowl and work it with your hands until smooth. Roll the dough into balls the size of a walnut.

Put the flaked almonds on a plate. Dampen the balls with wet hands and roll them around on the plate, pressing until they are covered in little shards of almond. Keep them in the fridge until you need them.

Note: You could turn these into super-food protein balls by adding 3 tablespoons of chocolate-flavoured protein powder – choose a high-quality one that doesn't contain any soy, gluten, dairy or GMO.

STAR ANISE AND CAYENNE PEPPER TRUFFLES

∼∽∽

BLOWING DANDELION

This is not just a truffle of originality, but also the holy grail of vegan food: a dairy-free truffle! Using coconut oil is a bit of a stroke of genius from Blowing Dandelion's Michaela: it melts into the chocolate almost on contact so there's much less risk of the mixture splitting, and as well as the lovely faint coconut notes in the flavour it gives an incredible smoothness to the texture. Flavour-wise, the warming star anise hits you first, then comes the surprisingly subtle fire of the cayenne. It's really very delicious.

Makes about 45

- 500g 67 per cent dark chocolate, Madagascan if you can get it
- 100g coconut oil
- 3 teaspoons star anise powder
- 1 teaspoon cayenne pepper
- 50g cocoa powder

Line a shallow 20cm square tray with greaseproof paper.

Break the chocolate into pieces and place in a heatproof bowl set over a pan of simmering water. Allow the chocolate to melt slowly over a low heat – don't stir it as the chocolate may seize. When the chocolate is completely melted, take the bowl off the heat and add the coconut oil, star anise and cayenne. Stir the unctuous mix gently until a drop put on your top lip or the inside of your wrist feels cool – i.e. test the temperature as you would a baby's milk bottle!

Pour the mixture into the lined tray and put it into the fridge until set. Either use a big, sharp knife to cut it into cubes or shards, or roll the mixture into balls between your palms. Toss the finished truffles in the cocoa powder and enjoy.

WATERMELON JUICE

❧

TURNIPS

Watermelon juice is one of those fantastic non-recipes: a deep pink blush, tasting even more of watermelon than watermelons do. A real blast of summery goodness, and always a lovely sight outside the Turnips shop in Greenwich.

Serves 1

• 1 large slice of watermelon

Cut the juicy pink flesh of the watermelon into chunks and discard the rind. Throw the chunks into a blender, then pour the juice through a sieve to get rid of the pips.

Bingo.

INDEX